Shining Through The Darkness

Steve Warren

Dedication

I dedicate this book to my parents, Robert and Marie Warren. I often say God gives us certain gifts at birth. There is no greater gift than having two extraordinary parents. My mother was strong-willed and lived a life devoted to her faith. She rooted herself in a firm belief in GOD and never wavered. My father was quite humble and gifted with common sense. Almost, I might add with a unique genius. His blue eyes would sparkle and shine every time he told us stories about his life. It is where my love of storytelling comes from. They both went into eternity many years ago. Often, I wonder what they'd think of how I turned out today. I am still the same person, but beneath the layers of my essence lies the faith-filled foundation they gave me. Thank you, Mom; thank you, Dad! I celebrate life because of you. With all my love, Steve.

Acknowledgments

To my dear friend, Romageane Personne, who has a rare ability to capture the essence of a photo and bring it to life! Thank you for taking the cover pictures for my book and giving me the permission to use them.

PROLOGUE

My favorite time of the day...when the first ray of sunlight illuminates my room. I awake as it permeates my mind and my being and covers me with warmth. Where light exists, hope exists! Somewhere in my soul, I know I came from light and will return to eternal light when God calls my name. Isn't this a remarkable gift? When we allow light to become a part of us, our essence will shine bright...so bright that others can see it and follow us. Anne Frank's diary described events that robbed her of a normal life. Her family went into hiding to avoid the fate of being sent to a concentration camp. A diary given to her for her birthday revealed the personal thoughts of a teenager growing up in confinement. Despite sufferings and ultimate death in Bergen-Belson, hope flickers on in the silence of her heart-to- heart words. My journal begins in February of 2020, the end of normalcy in America and in the world. COVID- 19 is the virus setting the stage now. "The only thing we have to fear, is fear itself" - Franklin D. Roosevelt's first inaugural address on March 4, 1933. Tough words to swallow during the peak of the Great Depression. And now, difficult words to digest in 2020. On May 8, 2020, the United States' unemployment rate hit the highest level since the Great Depression. Turn on the news and you can taste the fear in the air. Reporters revel in revealing facts and data in sensationalized formats. To be fair, they are attempting to unravel the mysterious virus, but blame accusations and character assassinations are rampant. So many unanswered questions swirl as the virus rears its ugly head. Heroes and survivors are depicted in the media along with individuals who lost their battle against this ruthless enemy! To quote Anne Frank: "In spite of everything, I still believe that people are really good at heart." It is difficult to build hope on a foundation consisting of confusion, misery, and death. Doctors, nurses, and hospital workers are understaffed and overworked. Gowns, masks, and ventilators are in demand with short supply. Once, when I was shopping in a grocery store before an approaching hurricane, a woman hollered out, "We're all going to die!" She was hysterically spouting doom and gloom, just like the story about Chicken Little. Fear is debilitating. It brings out hoarders, vigilantes, and unfortunately the worst in some people. Does anyone know who to believe or trust? Time to bring out our security blankets. Look at it this way: Despite everything, we need to keep moving. So don't linger in the path ahead. Move forward with faith and remember who is in control...GOD! Face it, kids: He's at the switchboard day and night. Trust your inner voice. Tackle life with a smile on your face. Shine on, brave warriors. God bless you in these perilous times!

So, when did the pandemonium start unravelling for me?

February 26th

Fears of the deadly virus have hit our shores; people are terrified to leave their homes without wearing masks. A horror film in the making; no one knows what to think. I do not want to hide in fear of what might happen. The rug is being yanked out from under our feet. Yes, bad things happen, but good things can also emerge from the bad. Anxiety, anyone? Read the paper or turn on the news! Who knows where this catastrophic event will take us! I wish we could step into a magical bubble and be shielded from the virus. Tomorrow, I plan to do everything to the hilt: sing, dance, and work in my yard - all of my favorite things.

My oldest son is moving into his new home and I am over the moon! Life goes on; we have to keep trucking.

My prayer today: Please, God, help us find a vaccine for this virus so the world can return to normal. No one should have to live in fear. Today at work, a precious baby smiled at me, and I see every reason for life to blossom forth. Embrace the cherished things in your life and SHINE!!!

March 1st a.m.

Whatever is in your life, whatever is not: Yesterday doesn't mean what you dream for today cannot be achieved tomorrow. Sow the seed of faith before taking your first step. Then water, wait, and proceed on to your next step. Patience is a virtue. One step, no matter how small, will propel you forward. We have been given the gift of TODAY, so Shine!!!

Footnote: LIFE IS LIKE BEING UP ON STAGE. When the sunlight emerges at dawn, go out and live joyfully with every fiber of your being. Make it an award-winning performance, even if you only have a bit part. LET YOUR STAR SHINE!!!

March 1st p.m.

This has been one ROCKY weekend, friends. Everywhere I look...problems. If I talk the talk (and I try), I must walk the walk. The road is rocky and full of potholes. In moments like this, take inventory. I am blessed with a well-stocked pantry: check. I am moving forward one foot at a time: check. Tomorrow is another day, and my message is: Decide what's important and claim it. Move on to a marvelous Monday and look for sunny skies. I plan on SHINING even through the clouds!!!

March 2nd

It's a cool evening tonight and crickets are chirping in my neighbor's tree. They love to party hardy! I found out that, according to something called Dolbear's Law, you can actually find out the temperature outside, and here's how: Count the number of a cricket's chirps in 14 seconds and add 40 to that number to get the temperature in Fahrenheit. Right now, I am looking up and see clouds moving across the night sky, and in the distance a star shines. Everything looks the same as it always has. But in my heart, I know it is not. Our world is topsy turvy with unpredictability because of the virus. My thoughts mirror the night clouds, swirling with uncertainty. So much weighing me down today. My dog is sick and has lost weight recently. Muffin has been my constant companion for many years now. Tomorrow she goes to the vet. Will she be able to hang on a little bit longer? Time is not her friend, nor is it mine. Yes, much is happening; life is shifting, re-arranging, and marching on. Some things we have power over, some we do not. Just like a reluctant child sent off to school, I have lessons to learn. Time for bed; the school bus will be here early. Shine on, my precious friends!!!

March 3rd

People are emptying the shelves in the grocery stores. Is Armageddon on the horizon? Scary, yes. If I started talking about Bible prophesies, many would tune me out. When you think it can't get much worse, suddenly you realize it can. Well, I'm not ready to move to a cave yet. When the sun is shining, I plan to be outside soaking it up. The Big Book reveals the love of many will grow cold. My advice: Warm things up! Love one another; keep an open heart, and don't give up the ship. Tomorrow is hump day, so stand up straight and SHINE!!!

March 4th

Today I encountered more panic in the streets. Reminds me of what happens during hurricane season in Florida. Thinking about what I may need to squirrel away before it arrives: water, canned goods, milk, money? Do you remember the 1960 movie, "The Time Machine?" In this movie, after a nuclear blast, people had to live underground and emerged as subterranean creatures called Morlocks. These creatures only came out at night. No, thank you. I prefer being a creature of light. Going into hiding does not suit me. Not a fan of stocking up on canned goods, either. But isn't it the unknown that scares us the most? Heck, to clear a path in a room now days all you have to do is sneeze and everyone will run for cover! The news reported that if you are over sixty, your risk of suffering with complications from the virus is not good. Three guesses on who they're referring to. Me! For now, business as usual. Remember to wash your hands. Like I said, time will tell. Off to dreamland. Tomorrow is Thursday, and my plan is to SHINE!!!

March 7th

We live in a must-do world, full of things that need attention, a world where the CLOCK rules. Today I don't want to do anything but relax. Doesn't everyone need a day like this? Slowing down thoughts in your brain isn't an easy thing to do. My favorite saying: "We are things of the day." Let this be a candy day: sweet, easy, good for the soul, and nourishing for the body. Skip the nourishing and hand me a candy bar...yum, yum, ready to Shine!!!

March 8th a.m.

Friends, I'm having so much fun in my second childhood. The more mellow I become, the less baggage I carry around. Less is better. I don't give a hoot or holler about what the critics think! My hope for each of you is to enjoy the sheer joy of being who you are without apologies.

A very special customer shops where I work, and she challenges me with old songs. It breaks the monotony of the day when we sing a few lines. For me, there is a magical connection when you sing, hear, and become the music. Another customer enjoys talking about cars. And a third likes to discuss recent books. Isn't it wonderful to share the gift of life? Be who you are; let your inner child out of the closet. Not everyone will get it, but BINGO, sometimes the right person does. Sharing makes life interesting and rewarding. Have fun when Monday arrives and SHINE!!!

March 8th p.m.

Even in the worst moments and situations, lessons are in sight.

Many are fearful about what might happen in LIFE. They forget we are only pilgrims passing through to the promised land. Storms are on the horizon again; people are hoarding supplies. Survival mode is in full swing. Friends, I understand the concern for what MIGHT come. But do you realize that GOD IS IN CONTROL? He never changes, nor does His Word. He will be with us till the end of time. Is this the end of time? I don't know; nobody on earth does. Outside my window, as I send you this message, a beautiful robin flew into my garden. The wind is wispy, and in the distance, it looks like rain. Life goes on with great anticipation. Possibilities exist every day. I am thankful for the opportunity to experience every second. I have a list, but FEAR is not on it. Happy Sunday! Live a life that Shines!!!

March 9th a.m.

What is the difference between who you are and who you desire to be? Perhaps drive, passion, and direction? Regardless of the circumstances, strive to become that person, for within each and every one of us lies the possibilities for greatness! Refuse to settle for anything less. I believe we have the ability to SHINE even through the darkness!!!

March 9th p.m.

A beautiful cool breeze swept through my great oak tree tonight.

I can see the full moon from my porch and hear fountains trickling in the nearby lake. Such a lovely picture. It seems impossible that in this perfect setting storm clouds are brewing. The Bible says, "Everything that can be shaken will be shaken."

Topics generating in the news: health, finance, unemployment, and anxiety about the disappearance of toilet paper. (Obviously the stock to buy before the pandemic). Who would believe it would come down to this? If only I could wake up and discover that this was just a bad dream. I'm here and you're here, and there is hope for another day to make a brand-new dream come true. Shine!!!

March 10th

I believe we are on earth to learn lessons. The universe presents us with daily opportunities in the class of "Life." Struggles with other people's behavior is probably at the top of the list of things I need to work on…a course of study in patience, tolerance, and kindness. I was watching a news report on TV when one person became so angry with another that he invited the other person to meet outside to settle the argument. How many times has someone brought you to anger? I understand, oh too well, because it has happened to me. This could be our SHINING moment to refrain, restrain, and not complain. Rise above the incident and you will pass the class of tolerance with flying colors. Not an easy lesson. I have failed more than I wish to admit, but I am doing better. Become the best person you can be. A better tomorrow is the reward. You can ace this as you Shine on Wednesday!!!

March 11th

A return to panic and fear as people emptied the shelves in grocery stores. Toilet paper was the first product to disappear. Guess one could say something's ready to hit the fan! To hoard or not to hoard? Inside my heart I hear a song: "What the world needs now is love, sweet love. No, not just for some, oh, but for everyone!" Don't be fearful, desperate, or angry. Be thankful for what you do have. My life is blessed, and I consider myself to be a rich man. Show kindness to everyone you come into contact with. Many noble people have been stepping up to the plate these days. What do you value at the end of the day? For me, it's my family and friends and my wonderful recollections of those who have passed over into the light. Celebrate and appreciate life on this radiant Thursday. Go out into the light and SHINE!!!

March 13th

These are disturbing days, my friends. Many expect MAN to uncover the answers. Yesterday, a wonderful lady was telling me that her choice for a political leader had a perfect plan. Well, I smiled and thought about it. I, too, have a political leader who I feel is doing everything possible to lead us. HOWEVER, dear friends, our leaders are men and women of flesh. Each one in their own way want to discover the answers to our problems. We, the people, need to call on GOD. If we humble ourselves as a nation and ask the Father for help, it will come. Why are we running around like chickens with our heads cut off? Shouldn't we be sprinting toward the One who never changes, the Great I Am? At the moment, I'm at the wheel, so permit me to say everyone needs to come together as one, no matter what party you back. United we stand, divided we fall! Like I used to tell my children when they were young: "Kids, you can fight later. Right now I need everyone on board." Peace and love to each of you. SHINE ON!!!

March 15th a.m.

I'm on a ROLL! Can't help myself; my mind is in the toilet. The term WIPE-OUT has a brand-new meaning. A little birdie said they are moving gold out of Fort Knox and replacing it with toilet paper. No longer a gold standard; it's a toiletry standard. Next in line, a lottery scratch off ticket: The Toilet Paper Jackpot Extravaganza. Scratch and win a year's supply of your favorite toiletry. In the bridal registry, the most sought-after gift is toilet paper; you've got to be kidding! Casinos are replacing slot machines with toilet paper symbols instead of cherries. Instead of "Hand over your money," thieves are demanding, "Hand over your toilet paper." Don't forget to laugh; it's good medicine. Shine, shine, shine!!!

Footnote: Hilarious survey when adding up your net worth: "How much toilet paper do you own?" Advice: If you want to quickly advance to the front of the line, cough out loud, sneeze, and you'll clear the deck fast. Forgive me, but it is just for laughs.

March 15th p.m.

Went to lunch today with friends. An older lady sat next to us. The establishment was almost empty. I was expecting someone would join the lady, but nobody did. She chatted into our conversation and told us she was lonely. Touched my heart, because if she had mentioned this earlier, I would have said, "Let's move our tables together." God created us to support each other, yet in this great vast planet so many are lonely. Do you remember these words from a famous song, "People who need people are the luckiest people I know?" Now with this despicable virus, everyone is reluctant to approach or touch one another. So we, who choose to SHINE, will work even harder to smile. Be congenial; cherish those around you! Sending positive thoughts to all of you! SHINE ON, MONDAY!!!

March 16th

Today is my birthday. The sky is beautiful, the sun is shining, and birds are singing. But right now, our world is in the most frightful place of my lifetime! I keep thinking and wishing, if only this had never happened. Hit erase, hit rewind, hit fast forward. But we can't. No guarantees about the future. Still, my mind is on overload. Panic again today; the "what might happen" attitude flared up again. My heart goes out to everyone in the business world. People are in jeopardy of losing their jobs. God help us! But here I am singing away and working as if it's a happy-go-lucky world. Friends, we have a choice. Nothing is more important than having our friends and loved ones around us. When we do, we are rich beyond all measure. For when we have, give, and receive love, it is beyond compare. Does anyone remember an old movie called "Hurry Sundown?" I'm ready for another day. Plan on surrounding yourself with the people dearest to you. Find your joy, rely on your strength, and you will SHINE!!!

Footnote: "Hurry Sundown" is a movie that came out in 1967 and was directed by Otto Preminger. Actors Jane Fonda and Michael Caine were the main characters. A controversy surrounded its theme, but I liked the song recorded by Peter, Paul and Mary, "Hurry sundown, be on your way. Weave me tomorrow out of today."

March 17th

Poor Saint Patrick (my patron saint) took a back seat to the "blank" this year. Can't bring myself to say the word! Not much fanfare, wearing green or talk of parties. Instead, anxiousness and dread has crept back in - lock, stock, and barrel. Do not make yourself sick by speculating about the future. Tough day trying to wear a smile at work, and even more difficult to have someone return one. Now is the opportunity to connect with loved ones. Come on, gang, bring out the games, puzzles, and movies. Hunker down, make oatmeal cookies, and pop some popcorn. Chill baby; make the best of a terrible situation. Shine on, Wednesday!!!

Footnote: One legend associated with St. Patrick: He drove all the snakes out of Ireland into the sea. If only he could do the same for COVID-19!

March 18th

Why don't we, as a nation, come together to PRAY for our country and the world by asking GOD to heal us? America has had a glorious run of prosperity and blessings in our lifetime. I remember my dad telling me about how my grandparents survived the Great Depression with very little. They counted their blessings and trusted that life would get better. Today, I think about all the modern conveniences that make our lives easier. My grandparents lived in a time when a toaster was considered a luxury. FRIENDS, Understand that this, too, shall pass. We can pull through this! Despite everything, we are richly blessed. Hope your day is topnotch. Put your toaster on light. Burnt toast is a terrible way to start the day. Don't forget to SHINE!!!

March 19th

Exhausted beyond belief. Want a challenging workout? Try working at a grocery store these days. People are anticipating stay-at-home orders. Given the chance, I might jump at the offer. Four words I could live without hearing over and over again are where's the toilet paper? My advice to chickens everywhere: Run for your lives! Grocery carts are being disinfected one minute and stockpiled with food the next. When this is over, I may need an extended vacation. Might find me making wicker baskets in my spare time. Place your orders now. Trying to be positive and helpful, but it's not easy. Someone complained (meant well, I'm sure) telling me I needed to keep a six-foot distance. How about six miles! Love you, mean it. Hope you have a fabulous Friday. I'm off to Shine!!!

March 20th

It's so profound: We're in a political season and society is demanding answers from MAN. Yes, GOD has appointed man to govern the earth, but it is a colossal mistake to believe a mortal man alone can solve the dire situation we are in. Let's try praying and asking God to impart wisdom to the men and women who will lead us into the future. Remember after 911, churches were filled to the brim. Weeks later, empty seats started reappearing. Mankind has become so intelligent (so they say) that they believe they have all the answers, which is a simple and maybe overzealous perception. Even the greatest scholar knows nothing before GOD. Friends, please stay close to our heavenly Father. Lean on him; difficult days are yet to come. So keep your eyes on God and your hearts full of love. Let's make tomorrow a super Saturday and SHINE!!!

March 21st

Sad news about the death of Kenny Rogers. I am a big fan. My favorite song of his is, "Just dropped in to see what condition my condition was in." Well, right now my condition stinks. Everything is headed downhill. Take my appearance: I look like "The Creature from The Black Lagoon!" On the outside, unshaven, unkempt and definitely not a fashionista. But wait - on the inside, I am stirring up an internal house-cleaning. Isolation is tough. What better time than now to contemplate on body, mind and soul? Life on planet Earth is precious. I've been thinking about friends and loved ones who have died. I'd like to talk to them and gain insight into what they learned on the other side. Perhaps they might say, "Cherish the little things in life." Remember, your bigger picture may not be God's bigger picture. These are my conditions, and I am dropping in to take serious inventory. Quiet meditation might help to free my mind of the clutter. Have a spectacular day. SHINE!!!

March 21st

It's surreal; evening arrived ever so softly. Slow-moving clouds cluttered the skies. A scattering of stars twinkled. The planes of existence once normal are not normal now. In my life, there is so much uncertainty. How can I assure my family that life will settle back down? Will I be able to protect them, as I feel it is my duty? I have to make changes. Friends, you must too. Who knows what direction this pandemic is heading in? One thing I know for sure is our patience is coming under fire. Gotta be strong! We are traveling down roads that have an abundance of detour signs. No other choice but to change our route. Keep on trucking and BELIEVE that we will find a way out of this maze. Hang in there; we'll talk tomorrow. Know that with faith and hope in our hearts, this too shall pass! SHINE!!!

March 22nd

Today I had nowhere - nowhere - to go, but I got up, cleaned up and dressed up! Do I fear anything today? Actually, I fear everything. I worry about becoming an old man who shuffles around at home wearing a tattered bathrobe and looking like Methuselah. Today, the family cat came across the room and looked at me like, what the hell happened to you? Thank goodness I have a few home projects calling my name, staying busy in any way I can: gardening, reading, and listening to music. Hey, the sun is surrendering and night's rehearsing. What will Monday bring? Goodbye fear; stop knocking on my door. Tomorrow I am going to SHINE!!!

March 23rd

The morning LIGHT is streaming through my window. The world is still alive. My heart soars for what might be. I look for possibilities in every moment. Was this fated to happen? Maybe. Despite my personal dilemmas, it's up to me and it's up to you on how we will handle this situation. If I can SHINE on good days, I can SHINE on bad days. Think about it: when love grows, fear shrinks. A quote by Etienne de Grellet: "I shall pass this way but once; any good that I can do, or any kindness I can show, to any human being, let me not defer nor neglect it, for I shall not pass this way again." Sending love & prayers to each of you. Keep on Shining!!!

Footnote: Psalm 118: "This is the day the LORD has made. Let us rejoice and be glad."

March 24th

To sum my world up in a single word: DISCIPLINE! I've put my part-time job (which I love) on hold. My GYM has closed, and my life has come to a screeching halt. AMAZING how our lives can change in a heartbeat! I am creating a new routine and trying to make the best of it. I hate being a house-bound person. Sometimes the cards don't fall in your favor. I'm not alone, but it's like being in detention. Can't say that I don't have time because I am doing time. How are you doing? Want to pass GO and get back to LIFE? What about "MONOPOLY?" I need the "Get out of jail card" before I play "Candy Land."

Easter is hopping around the corner, a wonderful excuse to devour a chocolate bunny! Discipline, oh discipline, where are you? Haven't a CLUE. Wait, that's another game. Whew, it's almost Wednesday. SHINE ON!!!

March 25th a.m.

Keeping a promise, is anything more important? Especially when you make a promise to yourself. I love the saying, "Tough times don't last, but tough PEOPLE do." Friends, these are excellent days to make promises to yourself. Strive to be an improved person. Do not let this barrier defeat you; conquer it! Today I've made a mental list of things I want to accomplish. Come on, join me! This situation does not control how you react to it. Each day is a precious gift. March forward with drive, purpose, and gusto! We will SHINE LIKE NEVER BEFORE!!!

March 25th p.m.

Today I came across a beautiful butterfly on my lawn. It was struggling and had surrendered to the ground beneath it. I picked up the magnificent creation and laid it on a statue wondering if butterflies experience fear or pain. Aren't our beginnings a little similar? Cocooned in the womb, propelled into the world, blooming forth and enjoying time in the garden. I can't believe how fast time has come and gone in my life. Colors once luminous seem to be fading. The clock is tick, tick, ticking along. I value my life here on Earth and plan on appreciating the time I have been given, just like the lovely butterfly. Fly high with glorious colors every chance you get. Have a terrific Thursday. Shine bright in your garden of life!!!

March 26th a.m.

Dear friends: Do something, keep busy, spruce up, LOOK UP. The mind is a complex computer, always working even if we aren't. Thinking too much is not good. Do not open the "what-might-happen" file. Instead, click the "activities" file. My plan: paint the house, mow the lawn, and listen to music. Control what you can. So let it roll (not toilet paper) and find a goal. SHINE BRIGHT!!!

March 26th p.m.

I always say it: Where did the day go? Today, time flew like a bat out of hell. After the everyday mundane work around the house, I tackled painting – no, not pictures but interior doors. I miss my social life big time. Went out to shop and discovered life is still revolving but at a slower pace. We must keep going. My little dog's health is so-so; she has good days and bad days. The medication the vet has her on makes her hungry 24-7; I can relate. Sometimes she follows me around, hoping I might drop some food from my plate. I am clumsy, and who knows better than my little shadow! Have a good night. Looking forward to Friday. Shine!!!

March 27th

Have you ever received a profound message in a dream? I received one last night in a series of scenarios. The recurring theme dealt with fears I've had in my life. In each story, I was anticipating a terrifying ending, but as I was guided through them, a sense of calm swept over me, and to my surprise, each scenario ended in victory. When I awoke, it hit me in the gut. Shouldn't we expect victories in life? Why do we train our minds otherwise? Kick your negative thoughts to the curb and embrace your positive ones. On earth, there is sorrow and sadness, but there is also love, joy and happiness. I remember when my old truck needed the radiator flushed out. Sometimes we need to flush out our thought processes and replace them with fresh, optimistic thoughts. Start out by repeating small affirmations: I think I can, I know I can, I knew I could! Set yourself up for victory and you will Shine!!!

March 28th a.m.

When you realize how little you know, then you will grow. There is more to life than we will ever understand. It amazes me, the sheer arrogance of people who puff themselves up because they feel that through extensive education, or because of a title, they possess all the answers. This universe we live in is too vast to imagine. Man - a speck in the galaxy, vain as a peacock. Keep your minds open and be willing to learn. Accept and treat each other with respect. From greatest to least, we are all in the same classroom together. Lessons are everywhere; we are in one now. Pay attention and SHINE!!!

March 28th p.m.

COVID-19 has turned our world upside down! People thought they were in control of their lives. Not now. "There's a kind of hush all over the world today" was a sweet song from the past. It's not about me or you, but everyone. With horror-stricken disbelief, I watch the news and it blows my mind. The U.S. is at the top of the list for the number of confirmed cases of the virus with Italy not far behind. Quarantined inside, there is an eerie HUSH in the streets. My mind goes back to when people had to go into hiding to escape the enemy, like Anne Frank. She kept her mind busy waiting for her life to return to "normal." Normal may not be materializing for months or perhaps years. Until then, I will keep reading, working out, and gaining knowledge bit by bit.

Quote from Ralph Waldo Emerson: "What lies behind us and what lies before us are tiny matters compared to what lies within us."

Hang in there and keep SHINING!!!

March 30th

We cannot go out to dinner, get our hair cut at the salon, go to the gym, or get together with family and friends we love. So what can we do? Stop complaining. Accept our circumstances at face value. Empower ourselves with positive thoughts, make goals, prioritize things you could not find the time to do yesterday. Tomorrow I will tackle my bathroom closet shelf by shelf. I already painted the doors - now on to the real nitty gritty. Being home is not my bag, but sometimes you need to clean out your bag. Make every second, minute, and hour count. This isolation will not last forever. There is a silver lining to everything. We will reach the finish line. And when we do, the inner strength gained from this situation will overcome any defeats. You never know what treasures lie inside your closet. Tuesday is almost here; don't forget to SHINE!!!

April 2nd

I'm fond of famous quotes and sayings, and one of my favorites would be "Every ending is a new beginning." Who doesn't want the virus to end? So how do we navigate through this calamity? I am in deep thought as I stare out my window. I see greenery and sunlight streaming through the room. Life continues at a standstill. Try to find a silver lining in this situation. Since we are "doing time" (so to speak), seize and clarify new tactics. TIME to consider other avenues. Tally up the pluses and eliminate the minuses. If we need to lose weight, do it. If we need to weed and plant, go at it! Damn it, get up and DO something. Yes, times are tough, but man, I'm dreaming of some new beginnings. Something good is on the horizon. I can feel it in my bones. SHINE ON!!!

Footnote: Lockdown is like being on spring break and our parents took the keys to the Thunderbird away!

April 4th

Days are running into each other; it is an eerie feeling. My dog is in seventh heaven because everyone is home, and she is basking as the center of attention with treats, walks, etc. But…she has also become more demanding. I, on the other hand, feel like I am stuck on a deserted island and trying not to eat my way out of here. Limiting the time I spend watching the news to stay positive. Mind over matter - easier said than done! Often hopeful, but other moments wondering if life ever be the same again. I'm a lucky guy because the positive thoughts always win. I nod respectively to the fridge and pantry as I pass by. Keep moving, Warren! Try to Shine every moment of the day!!!

April 6th

I love an excellent play just as much as the next. But this virus is not a play. We have to stop the drama. Do what you're told to do. Didn't our mothers tell us that? Stop the complaining. Almost everyone is out of work. But the media is going into overtime. Like it or not, our president has surrounded himself with the top in their profession. The doctors are telling us the facts as they realize them. But like an unwelcome guest, we can't wait until we no longer have to see or hear them on the news. WE want this nightmare to go away! Until then, please do your best with dignity and grace. I don't want to fear dying. Even worse, I don't want to fear living. I believe GOD has a plan for us and I'm putting my trust in it. Please, God, shed your light on all the sick and suffering families. I'm praying for them; that's in my power, the rest is not. Stay strong, never give up and SHINE!!!

April 7th

God created life to keep moving. The sun comes up, the moon goes down, clouds change, the wind blows and the tide rushes in and out. Friends, we are a part of this sublime movement. I'm going with the flow. A person declared that life has stopped. No, it's moving. Reminds me of the times I went down a river in a float…passing through, hanging out, along for the ride. That is what we are doing now. Even this situation cannot stop movement. The wonderful news: there is a shore. We will get there. Don't look back. Keep your eyes fixed on searching for the shore. SHINE on, sailors!!!

April 10th a.m.

This morning I replied to a wonderful woman's post about life. It was my response related to a job (patient escort) I had in a hospital and the precious people I met. I cannot recall the young black woman's name, but her image lives on in my heart. She appeared soft- spoken and kind despite being in pain. My assignment was to bring her to the surgery floor. Quite possibly, I connected with her gentle spirit because we were about the same age. Sadly, she died soon after. The reason I'm telling this story to you is because I learned a valuable lesson: Appreciate this journey called LIFE. Some people experience a brief period on earth. TIME is a most exquisite and valuable gift. Don't waste a moment in hatred, scorn or contempt. This gift is a loan; treat it with respect. I am perplexed about how some people live their days at odds with their fellow man. Work on practicing humility. At any second it might be "lights out." Live with gusto, joy and respect in each moment. Discover your gifts, sprinkle love around, and you will SHINE!!!

April 10th p.m.

I hope you realize by now that I am a positive person most of the time. The ball (as they say) is in your court. You can decide to be a positive person or a negative one. Circumstances may try to sway your mental attitude; don't allow it. Peace disseminates inside our souls when we snuff out conflict. Everyone around the world can't wait for these grueling days to be over. So how are you choosing to live through them? I've seen the best come out in people. Most are stepping up to the plate, being polite and helpful. I have faith in mankind. As always, there are exceptions, but I feel hope circulating, and it is a wonderful thing. Will our troubles end soon? I would love to tell you yes, BUT this place we dwell in is filled with uncertainty. Ground yourself with faith and love, knowing this is only a pit-stop. Wave your flag high as you get back into the race! Ready, set, go. Shine; it's almost Saturday!!!

Footnote: "Hey Lefty, just wait till we break outta of this joint. Man, we going to paint this town!" Dialog from an old prison movie? No, me talking to the dog this morning. Will someone please bake me a cake with a file in it? Shine on, shiners!!!

April 11th

"People who need people are the luckiest people I know." Who remembers this famous tune? I do and I'm living it. Isolation is not my cup of tea; even the dog is sick of hearing my stories (she's hiding under the bed). Our Easter plans were canceled; so sad! But I believe we will make it out of this black canyon with a greater appreciation of the hustle, bustle and sounds of life. I saw a picture of a New York street and it reminded me of the movie, "On the Beach." Life should not be like this. I want to wish each and every one of you a HAPPY EASTER. With a song in our hearts, we will beat this rap! Got to go find my dog. "Muffin, come out from under the bed; I have another story to tell you." SHINE ON!!!

Footnote: "On the Beach" – a 1959 post- apocalyptic science fiction movie. This black- and-white film was based on a book with the same name. Setting: 1964 following World War III. The cast included: Gregory Peck, Ava Gardner, Fred Astaire and Anthony Perkins.

April 12th

When I was young, Easter was about candy, coloring eggs and having a large family dinner. Yes, church was definitely on the agenda. Our mother explained why Christ had to die to atone for our sins, but my childish mind was on the festivities. I suppose age and experience led me to realize man needs a savior. Still, the Bible passage that says "No one is righteous, no, not one" bothered me. I considered myself to be an upright person. But deep down in the heart of humans lies the opportunity for mass destruction. We pop out of the womb needy and demanding; it's in our nature. Perfection is not in the plan. Many false "saviors" show up from time to time trying to turn our heads. In the world today, mankind often makes the mistake of not embracing the Ten Commandments. God states the rules plain and simple but lots of people are looking for loopholes. When we put faith in men and women who believe that the end justifies the means, we are in deep trouble. Sometimes it's like we are in the back seat of a fast-moving car (life), feeling powerless. Who is your driver? I am not a gifted preacher or evangelic, but when peace and love is in my heart, I know firsthand that it is amazing! JESUS LIVES and is beyond anything we have or can experience here. HAPPY EASTER TO EACH AND EVERY ONE OF YOU. HE SHINES AND SO CAN YOU!!!

April 13th a.m.

Made it through another humdrum weekend. An uneventful trip to the dump was the highlight of my work week. I tackled some mean bougainvillea plants that were in need of trimming. The world looks the same from my truck window, although there are not as many vehicles on the road. Simple acts we took for granted are cherished now. The news is talking about opening the country back up. America closed for business; will things return to normal? When we hear someone sneeze or cough, will our eyes open wide or will we return to hugs or {gulp} shaking hands? Adjustments in the new normal, for sure. Things may be awkward, but who knows...perhaps the old vintage peace signs will make a comeback! Peace, baby, peace. Shine on, Tuesday!!!

April 13th p.m.

Both my dog and I had a difficult night. Her tiny body is failing. Not in pain, but very restless. At 2 a.m., she got up and paced the floor looking for food. Then she signals she needs to go potty. If only I could wave a magic wand to make her young again. For her, twilight is approaching. The timing is difficult to grasp when everyone on earth is struggling to find the light. Quarantine plays with our minds. It's like opening a dusty room and you can't breathe. The road is rocky; lots of bumps. If we follow the yellow brick road, will we find our way back? I hope so. Chores are calling. So, I will hug my little dog tight as we both go outside to begin a new day. Shine!!!

April 14th a.m.

Another day is on the horizon. Please recognize it's possible to become a better person than you were yesterday. Seize the opportunity and stake your claim! Maybe you weren't kind enough, thoughtful enough, and made some mistakes. Fix the ones you can; erase the ones you can't. We don't have the power to change other people, but with GOD we can change ourselves! Believe in yourself; the sky is the limit. Shine on!!!

April 14th p.m.

Thunder, lightning and much needed rain tonight. Similar to my world. This has not been a pretty season. It has been filled with storms and unrelenting rain. Most likely the vet will put my sweet dog Muffin to sleep tomorrow. Her health is going downhill; she is not eating and is in pain now. It's difficult to tell you just how I feel cause I'm not sure myself. She has had a wonderful life, adored and cherished. Yes, death is part of life but now it is everywhere I look. Dreadful news and uncertainty lurking around every corner. My mind can't find rest. I am clutching to the phrase "this can't last forever" and depending on it too. Today I decided I will return to my part-time job. Even with all the risks, I can't lock myself away. For me, it's best to be out with other people (even if it's at a six- foot distance and wearing a mask). Wherever this life is going, I have to keep moving. My advice: Try not to let the worries of the world devour you; take one step at a time. There is a season for everything. I pray we can find our way towards a better and kinder one. Things will return to a new normal. The rain has stopped; it has refreshed the earth. Keep moving toward the light so we can Shine!!!

Footnote: Our precious Muffin passed over the Rainbow Bridge on 4-15-20. My sister, Dee, drew this portrait weeks before we even knew she was sick. Shine on, my sweet girl!!!

April 16th a.m.

The definition of opportunistic: Exploiting chances offered by immediate circumstances without reference to a general plan or moral principle. People are pointing fingers about who to blame for the havoc of the pandemic. Everything happening goes against our very being. God created man to live in social harmony and to enjoy each other's company. There is magic in human touch. The enemy devises to divide and conquer. Who is the enemy? You decide; I already have. I'll spare the details. The wonderful news is that this too shall pass...I know, I know, I said it again. Bear with me and turn this time into a positive opportunity for growth and learning. Hit the pause button. Decide where you are going from here. Take a deep breath and exhale.

One of my favorite movies is "The Grapes of Wrath" based on the novel written by John Steinbeck, a story about a family that tries to stay afloat during the depression. At the end of the movie, the father has been beaten down with defeat. But the mother (who reminds me much of my late mother) finds her strength and steps forward to say, "They can't wipe us out; they can't lick us." We ARE the people, and this can't keep us down! Better days are coming with opportunities to prosper. Have a blessed day and SHINE!!!

Footnote: There are some days that I relate to how people must have felt to be knocked down during "The Great Depression." People did not know which way to turn. So too are the times we live in today. No one can tell us when the pandemic will end. We must rely on Spiritual COURAGE to persevere these uncertain times!

April 17th

How does one find out what "they are made of?" In life, sometimes you discover it at your own pace. Other times, a situation dumps a heaping serving of life on your plate. I've seen an awe-inspiring amount of caring and goodwill during this pandemic. Despite social distancing, people are reaching out. HOPE! Latch on to the bandwagon! Anyone who has felt they haven't done enough? Now is your chance. Life can't be about me. It's about US, striving to help each other. Everyone in the universe is mystically connected; it's in our DNA. Shine on to a sensational Saturday!!!

April 19th a.m.

Living in the pandemic has discombobulated my sleeping patterns. Staying up late reset my inner clock, but my dreams have been appearing in full force. There is a question that I have always wondered about: Can the dead communicate with us? Last night, a friend who died years ago materialized. I'd often had fond memories of her, and to converse with her was mind boggling. She wanted me to know how happy she was in the afterlife. But when I awoke, a deeper message emerged. True power lies in our mind's ability to filter out negative thoughts. Just the other day, a stranger in line was talking with me and wishing ill on people he was holding accountable for the country's predicament. We will only provide fuel for the fire if we surrender to negative patterns. Do we allow the world to fall deeper into despair by allowing our minds to draw it there? Something to think about. The sheer power of thought is like an unbridled horse running wild. The lesson here may be in the power that each one of us possess. Use your power wisely! I did not know the man in line, but I told him I wished the best for everyone. He looked at me like I was a crazy person. But I own my thoughts; I choose them to be genuine. Yeah, sometimes it takes work, but I want to live in peace. I hope you will too. Be mindful of one another, continue with positive intentions, and SHINE!!!

April 21st

Every day has its challenges, but may I add, so blessed are we who have them. I like myself best when I am conscious of all my blessings. They flood my life like a bright light. My weaknesses are re-enforced when I compare my life to others. That, my friends, has been my biggest flaw. Being aware of it fills me with contemplation. Sadly, sometimes I place importance upon the wrong things. Granted, I'm still a work in progress, but then again, aren't we all and isn't it our greatest mission? Like who you are. Trust who you are. Share who you are and practice with great authenticity! Time to fix one of my toilets. Lofty ambitions as I plan to SHINE!!!

April 22nd a.m.

I encountered a discouraged person who said to me, "I need a reason for hope." Amid these grueling days, I understand, so here is my answer: Let LIGHT be the reason. Light alone? Yes. Edith Wharton, American novelist, said it best: "There are two ways of spreading light: to be the candle or the mirror that reflects it." Every day look for the light; BE THE LIGHT and SHINE!!!

April 22nd p.m.

To stay locked down or not locked down? Does anyone know the best answer? Not me. Today I had to go out, and it was a refreshing change. It's strange going into familiar places with different rules. People pass by in masks, and I feel like I am in an old episode of "The Twilight Zone." At any moment I'm expecting a flying saucer to land. Even my family seems on guard when I return. What will I miss in this sterilized world? The spontaneity of a random hug or touch? Remember the movie, "The Boy in The Bubble?" He longed to leave his germ- free environment. That is one bubble I would love to bust. Step out to a wonderful Wednesday and SHINE!!!

April 23rd a.m.

Good morning, everyone! Finished watching an old sitcom from the 1960s. It was silly, corny and outright DELIGHTFUL! Don't want to knock anyone's taste in entertainment but they flood TV today with tragic dramas. I miss the silly. The world needs innocent silly moments to just laugh. People may say that's not reality. What about you? I've had my fill of reality. Anyone out there miss easy breezy shows like HEE HAW? We all need a break from the news. Find something to make you smile and laugh today. Laughter helps boost your immune system. Good for the mind, body and soul. SHINE!!!

April 23rd p.m.

The Man Behind the Mask. Sound like an old movie? Nope, just sums up my work life these days. Trying to be the real me, but it's difficult living behind a mask. People have been polite. I think most everyone is trying to be a dutiful citizen. Many stores around us are closed; it's surreal, almost like walking through a lovely forest, but sheets of plastic are obscuring the views. Signs everywhere read, Do Not Touch! Reminds me of a visit to a beautiful home where the hostess allows you to sit on a couch covered in plastic (whoosh). You look up and see her please-do-not-touch-anything face. I'd rather be at home sitting on a comfortable weather- beaten sofa. Shine on to Friday!!!

April 25th a.m.

I HAVE learned many lessons in my lifetime. The most noteworthy is to be yourself! Embrace what you see in the mirror. The freedom of making life choices is yours and yours alone. What alarms me is how fast people are allowing others to control them in politics, faith and overall life. If a business opens and it scares you to go in, don't. But please don't stop me. Common sense and safety are of the utmost importance. No one wants to place themselves in danger. Life as we knew it will resume. I can't believe a political party is shunning a member because they thanked our president. Does anyone find this disturbing? Freedom is one of our most valuable gifts. Many have given their lives so we may live. Yes, we need to be careful and follow rules, just don't give up FREEDOM along the way. Come on! You can do it! Shine - Saturday's here!!!

April 25th p.m.

Has anything good resulted from this pandemic? For me, it's the stark realization of everything (spiritual as well as material) God has blessed me with. Don't know how blessings arrive, but I'm counting my blessings on all my fingers and toes. I say it all the time: "Thank you, GOD, for all I have, the people in my life, even the tough times, because they all brought me here. And here is the best place ever." Sure, there are precious moments that I can never re- live, but I can't lose sight of today by looking in the rear-view window of my life. I don't want fear invading thoughts of the future. I was fortunate to talk with a good and caring friend on the phone today. If you have one wonderful friend, you have hit the jackpot! Fear mongers say we will deplete our resources. Rely on faith. I experienced a day when everything looked impossible and I had one solid dollar to my name, but I was determined to keep going. Friends, despite everything, give praise each day and give the glory to GOD. Our lives are much like a book. Read this page today and the next page tomorrow. Don't zoom ahead, you might miss the best part. Hopping on to Sunday! Become a beacon of light and SHINE!!

April 26th

I don't know about you, but one of the worst things about being shut in is that you let your appearance slide. Sometimes I don't dress neat. I forget to shave, and as I pass a mirror, like I told you before, I look like the creature from the Black Lagoon - but it's me! The cool thing is no one cares. But if the doorbell were to ring, someone would scream. I do not want to be arrested for vagrancy at home. Even the cat is hissing. When I was a mailman, someone answered the door looking like Al Bundy...and now it's me. HELP! My plan is to clean up nice and sit down for dinner. "Can someone please pass the tea and crumpets?" Have a great rest of the day. Out of the lagoon for now. Almost Monday and I plan to Shine!!!

April 27th

It's true, the evil side recognizes your weaknesses. But truer, GOD is your strength and fortress. Thus - and above all else - call upon GOD for fortitude and believe that He will answer your call. Start your day with GOD and you cannot go wrong. He is the Master planner! SHINE in His glory!!!

Footnote: "He gives strength to the weary and increases the power of the weak." -Isaiah 40:29

April 28th

Serving the public is similar to attending college. A bonafide course in LIFE. You observe and hear more than you would like to. But wait - this is an advanced course. It requires diving below the surface. You assume this or that when you glance at a person, but it is only a scratch on the surface. One person displays airs of money, another good-looking person seems the most likely to succeed. And don't forget the frumpy-bumpy person who would never make the best-dressed list. Gaze beyond the facade and into their soul. What other people allow us to perceive, or limit us to knowing, is a fraction of who they are. I remember when I was a freshman in high school. I speculated about a classmate who appeared to have it all: looks, popularity, and brilliance - everything I wanted to be but felt I lacked. Envious, yes. Many years later, I found out he had committed suicide. Inconceivable but true. I wished I could have been his friend. The lesson is don't assume. Most people are dealing with issues, so look into everyone's heart and treat them as equals. Who knows? A frumpy-bumpy just might end up in the top of this class. There is hope. Signing off as a frumpy-bumpy soul who likes to SHINE!!!

April 29th

All the king's horses and all the king's men couldn't put Humpty back together again. Man, not surprising when they had to stay six feet apart. Going out in this unfamiliar world, surreal. Please practice kindness with the mandated orders. When arrows point which way to go down an aisle, follow them correctly. I don't know, maybe it's me, but many people furrow their eyebrows with mistrust. Makes me terrified to cough or sneeze for fear of the paddy wagon coming to take me away! And have you noticed on the roads that there seems to be an increase in aggressive drivers? Too much turmoil on people's minds today. But isn't the goal to make it to tomorrow? Just keeping that thought in my mind along with patience and mercy. It can't be easy for young families with obligations to meet. Everyone have a great THURSDAY. Safety first and foremost. Even with six feet apart distances, try to keep an open heart and you will SHINE!!!

April 30th a.m.

I find the human existence to be intriguing. People pass judgment upon one another as if they are authorities on all subjects. We see the results of people's actions but know little about what lies deep in one's heart and soul. We assume God's responsibilities when we become judge and jury. Yes, GOD is an enigma. It will shock many of us when He calls us into His office. I have a sneaking suspicion He differs from what we thought. I've never even seen His picture and I'm sure you haven't either. Friends, there are evil humans in our world from the very top to the rock bottom. It's vital to be aware of this, but don't let it destroy your goodness by seeing the darkness in them. They will take their turn in the office too. Thank goodness the Creator is both judge and jury. He will reveal all the answers; there will be quite a few pink slips handed out {gulp!}. Keep your heart pure and don't let anyone smother your light. SHINE on to Friday!!!

April 30th p.m.

Reflection for the day: No one likes pain. Today the world is in significant pain. Pesky thorns in our sides. We are all praying for a miracle. GOD does not think as we might expect. Sometimes He does not remove the thorns when we want Him to. He gives us strength to endure each day if we keep the FAITH! As most of you might know, I love gardening, and Bougainvilleas are my favorites. The colors that blossom forth are breathtaking, yet they have nasty thorns. Sometimes my arms look like I've tangled with unruly cats! Magnificence colors burst forth in our souls following the healing process. Let your colors SHINE forth, and so will your heart!!!

Footnote: It's not who you were, rather who you ARE today that counts. Grasp that with all your might. No rainbows in the sky? PAINT one. Rejoice in this day. Give your heart the right to soar with anticipation for what is coming! Apologies unnecessary; let go of negative thoughts. You are here for a reason. This little heart of mine, I am going to let it SHINE!!!

May 4th p.m.

A lot of talk about getting back to normal this week. Please let it be soon, God! Do we need to accept a new normal? Sometimes I feel like a spaceship has transported me to a different planet. At work everyone wears a mask, and it muffles the uplifting things I want to share: my smiles, laughter, and singing songs with people. Time to follow the rules, guys. We owe it to our fellow man, woman and child. Safety is paramount; insurrection has consequences. I am looking forward to my gym opening back up, even though I've established a routine at home. For now, that's where we are. Does a smile lurk beneath your mask? Soon our smiles will be set free and we will SHINE!!!

May 6th a.m.

Our lives, like the seasons, are changing and forever re-arranging. So many times we resist. Forever in spring, cool and crisp. Summer brings sunshine and a delightful time. Spectacular colors of fall, a kaleidoscope of awe. Winter not so much when Jack Frost nips us on the nose. The earth is mighty but must surrender and move on. For everything that showed up, and all that's gone, mere travelers have no choice but to submit. Seasons are fast paced, hold on to the lessons that you learned. Sometimes the path ahead is not easy to see or understand. Do not fear the unknown, bleak winds of a twilight zone. Wisdom comes when we accept and no longer run. Our hearts accept and sing. Welcome winter, spring, summer and fall, we relinquish to you all as we SHINE ON!!!

May 6th p.m.

Reported on the news tonight: Sunlight can kill the virus. I hope so! How many of us appreciate the power of a simple ray of light as the sun rises? I am no scholar, but my soul heals itself through the power of sunlight. Nothing is more electrifying as when the first light of the day comes forth, exploding its energy everywhere. My mother loved the seashore. At a very early age, she would load up the car, and off to the beach we'd go. The salty water and sunlight seemed to re-energize every cell in our bodies. On the way home, it felt as if the ocean and sun had cleansed our bodies. My sister used to sneak shells and ocean water home in her sand bucket. Our mother made her carry it to the backyard and she would run out and sniff the ocean smells as long as it lasted. Not trying to get mystical with you, but it's like our beings came out of the sunlight mixed with the ingredients of the ocean. My prayer is for summer to arrive with an overabundance of light. Go out, embrace it, and healing will spread throughout the land. Where there is LIGHT, there is hope. So, let your light SHINE forth. Hope can spread faster than any virus! So on to Thursday. Shine bright in the morning light!!!

May 8th

I will call this "The Quiet Time." I got to know someone up front and personal: me, myself and I. The world is often distracting with sights, sounds and movements everywhere. Then the virus dumped the unthinkable on our doorstep, and everything around us became quiet. One minute I find things to do, the next I don't. My mind reflects on my purpose in life. So, I am figuring out about what's important and what's not important, like cleaning clutter out of the garage - some things down to the curb. My heart soars for revitalizing territory! Friends, there are no guarantees. Who YOU are and what you believe is something no one can take away from you. You have an extraordinary power of being who you are and what God created you for. Isn't that wonderful?

Take advantage of your quiet time. What do you want to accomplish; what makes you happy? When the masks come off, show the world who you are with a magnificent smile and SHINE!!!

May 9th

Happy Mother's Day to all the ladies! My mother passed away many years ago - much too soon and way too young. I smile, remembering she was a force to reckon with. She met my father in Australia when he was stationed there during World War II. After a short courtship, they got married. And as the war was coming to an end, Mom traveled from Australia to America with my older sister to begin a new life. Arriving in an unfamiliar country without friends must have been scary. But with Mom's charismatic personality and Aussie accent, she soon had a multitude of friends. The couple settled into a home in south Florida when Pops got out of the Army. Three more children arrived, and Mom never looked back; she was a woman of FAITH with an unshakable Christian attitude. After she passed away, I was reluctant to talk about her with anyone. It was easier to block out memories I could not deal with. Often when someone dies, people try to comfort the loved ones. But grief for me seemed to have its own little compartment. My way to deal with it was to keep it hidden in a safe place. I can say, a mother - a wonderful one - cannot be duplicated. Life goes on, and I am finally in a place where I can take out that box and sort through my memories of her. Sometimes I wonder what she would think about my life now. I am not who I was then. Would she approve? Now that she resides in a perfect place, I believe she knows the entire story, both mine and hers. I miss you, Mom. Happy Mother's Day in Heaven! You live on in my heart where your memory SHINES!!!

Footnote: A picture of my parents, Mary Dorothea and Robert Preston Warren, taken in Australia during WWII.

May 10th

A few moments ago, while taking out the garbage, a light rain trickled down my forehead. I don't know how to explain, but it was soothing and purifying. The rain lifted a burden off my soul. Sound silly? I've been testing the value of being in the minute. We take so much for granted. If these unsure times are not reminding you, they should be. Before the virus slowed us down, all the wheels were turning fast. Then time paused and what had been is not. Friends, we all live in a world of insurance and 401k's. Planning the future is a good thing to do. Just don't plan on it being a forever thing. Nothing is forever. Enjoy the moment. Yesterday I spent time at the seashore where sights and sounds and the sun were holding court. I looked at the footprints in the sand and watched as the tide came rushing in and erasing them in a second. Look around at your loved ones and appreciate every moment with them. Choose LOVE over disagreements. Like the footprints in the sand, moments will disappear into eternity. I want to cherish every moment. Hope everyone had a great Mother's Day. It's only hours and minutes away from another day. SHINE and enjoy every moment!!!

May 12th

Man, many opportunists are out there taking advantage of the virus situation. I made a promise to myself when I started writing this post not to make it political. I try to stay out of that arena, but the handwriting is on the wall. SHAME on the people who are doing it for selfish reasons. A big shout out to the amazing humanitarians who strive to help those who can't go out in public. I've seen these heroes shopping and doing other types of chores for those who can't. Many times, I have heard someone say, "I wish I could do more." It doesn't have to be earthshaking. How about calling someone? Sometimes just a word of encouragement can make someone's day. Send a card in the mail. Even I (a former mail carrier) enjoy checking the mailbox for a surprise! No, we can't change the entire world. So what can we do? Seek the opportunity to act with kindness. When we SHINE, so do others!!!

May 13th a.m.

To be honest with you, I feel like the general media is playing dodgeball with my mind...and a rather mean-spirited game at that. Maybe it is just me, but they are spreading fear into our future, like mayonnaise on a slice of bread. This might be the worst winter. It might lead to this. The virus might cause this to never return. OK, it MIGHT. But I can't live in the what-might-happen business. Doesn't work for me. Yes, this is a baffling time, like none I've ever seen before (and - I hope - never again). No hiding in my room. Not telling you what to do. I am like a toddler, taking baby steps - one foot in front of the other. Ran some small errands today and ended up buying a plant that I've had my eye on. Followed the arrows and kept my distance. Tomorrow I look forward to working at my part-time job. I don't enjoy wearing a mask, but it is the right thing to do. My nose hurts, my ears hurt, and try stuffing a mustache into a small mask (think caterpillar). Not meaning to complain. Gotta do what I got to do. Please don't scare me about what might happen. I'm going out into the light! Make Thursday extra special. Shine underneath your masks!!!

May 13th p.m.

My topic for today: Things going bump in the night. I grew up living in an old wooden house. At night, all kinds of noises and creaks settled around the structure, most likely mice running around in the attic. The rear bedroom had a small panel in the ceiling; you could get into the attic if you moved it up. One of my older siblings told me that a monster lived in the attic. I refused to sleep in that room. Don't monsters eat small children? I was convinced - hook, line and sinker. There have been many bumps since then, but somehow, I survived. When I was searching for employment as an adolescent man, my fears escalated. Would I be able to acquire a superb paying job? Well, I found one – or, rather, GOD found one. Fears continued to pop up in my life. Then I heard a voice: "I am with you always." Yes, GOD has always been with me. Rugged days in 2020, wouldn't you agree? Pluses and minuses abound. Friends, fear is on a long vacation. It's parked itself smack dab in the middle of our planet. No pun intended, but fear is having a ball, and it's sending out invitations to everyone to join in. I rely on the voice I heard. I stand with it. GOD is, was, and has always been. Does this mean I will escape without a scratch? Can't say for sure, but I believe His will for my life is rock solid. Don't worry about things going bump in the night. Faith is the key; it unlocks many doors. Trust in GOD for everything in your life. Believe He will be right there at your side as long as you dwell on planet Earth. Walk with Him and attain the promise of a magnificent day when everything will be bright and beautiful. Heaven is the one place fear cannot maintain residence. Our Father has a majestic home waiting for those who love Him. It is a place where we will SHINE forever!!!

May 15th

Fear mongers have a lot to monger about amid this pandemic. "The sky is falling" rings from the rooftops. My heart breaks for those who depend on employment to pay the bills and bring home the groceries. I can't even imagine the worry. On one hand, some are begging for the country to re-open, followed by the cries of "It's too soon!" I don't know if it is too soon. For people struggling with keeping food on the table and a roof over their heads, maybe it's never too soon. I've ventured out in my neck of the woods following the rules to wear a mask where it's mandatory and washing my hands. I even change clothes in my garage before entering the house. I will not allow myself to slip into the place where fear lives. Saturday is almost here. Shine on, my friends. SHINE ON!!!

May 16th

Never take a single second for granted. Foster a desire to live with gusto! I recall, with love and sadness, family members and friends who have gone into eternity before me. Many of them departed at a much younger age than I am today. Life is such a precious, precious gift. During this shutdown, time has become of UTMOST importance to me. The sheer value of it…mind-boggling. It is time to organize your priorities like cleaning out the attic/garage/closet. Decide what you need and unload the baggage. Let your dreams soar and you will become the person you always wanted to be. There is plenty of time to accomplish your goals and SHINE!!!

May 17th

It was one of those days when nothing goes right. Into each life some rain must fall. Makes you appreciate when everything falls into place. I tried to take a deep breath and focus on staying calm. In with the good, out with the bad. Our AC unit, which is five years old, started acting up - something you dread in the Florida summers. A polite man arrived on Saturday to fix the unit. He later reported that everything checked out OK, but after he left, problems checked in again. Oh no, another uncomfortable night. I remember when my father purchased our first window AC unit. It did not cool the entire house, so I would stand in front of it on sultry nights. In those days, we lived in an old house that had a large attic fan. As I laid in bed at night, I could hear my father flick on the switch and an enormous WHOOSH sound sucked up the heat. Crime wasn't what it is today; we often left the windows open. The night sounds of frogs in the distance and whistle of a train pulling into the station was soothing. It's funny - once you have something, you can't imagine living without it. Go back to the good old days? Nah, I'll stick to today even though I will break out in a sweat tonight. FIX my AC, please! I will smile through the madness on Monday and SHINE!!!

May 18th a.m.

In the core of my heart, I believe each one of us is created "FOR A TIME SUCH AS THIS." (Esther 4:13-14). Our society has put too much importance on authorities. Yes, I understand that during these times we need experts telling us what to do and not do, but I've yet to hear them say anything about humbling ourselves and asking GOD to heal our lands. Friends - acknowledge the existence of our Creator. Ask Him to heal our lands, to keep us safe and bring us into salvation. Yes, listen to the experts. But we, who have faith, must realize that GOD and God alone can heal our land. Turn to Him and trust in His Word. I will go out on a dangerous limb and say only a fool will count on mankind, and mankind alone, to bring the recovery without God's help and intervention. We are in the midst of a frightful event. With God, we can rebuild and restore. FOR A TIME SUCH AS THIS, it is imperative to SHINE!!!

May 18th p.m.

Dear friends, I have been watching the series called "World on Fire." The show's setting is WW2 during the polish invasion. Horrific and sad things occurred during this conflict. The series is very profound, and I highly recommend viewing it. I've written this before and I stand by it: There is little hope for mankind itself, for society never seems to learn its lesson. But the glimmer of hope lives in the individual; it's the reason I work so hard to turn the rudder. Will we crash? Most likely. I believe that individuals exist who can and will bring hope for the future. For as long as faith, hope and charity prevail, we can find a path. Our energy will transform itself in the beautiful light of a beautiful dawn. I am not worried at all. How foolish is it to worry about what one's material legacy will be rather than making a conscious decision about leaving behind the essence of your soul and how you have touched someone's life. Keep your hearts pure. Focus on your purpose while treating others with respect and direct your attention to your purpose. We are only a second in eternity, so make that second count. SHINE on with extraordinary hope for tomorrow!!!

May 20th

I used to hear so much about the "ME" generation, and to be honest, it did a number on all of us! When I was a child, manners and etiquette were imperative. Next, the age of what's right for YOU came along. Yes, it's important to feel good about yourself, but never at the cost of another. Manners still count. I was forever telling my children that having good manners opens doors, and open doors lead to opportunities. I still believe that, and when I look at a polite child, I see a future success. Sayings that our parents used to say: "Elbows off the table" "Because I said so" "I'll wash your mouth out with soap" "Money doesn't grow on trees, you know." There were other important things they stressed like giving a seat to a woman or opening doors, but most of all was putting others before yourself. It could not be all about ME. When I was being my usual blabbermouth, I remember my mom saying, "Steve, there are other people in this room!" THERE are other people on this earth. We need to respect and make ROOM for them. Shine on!!!

May 21st

Weird feeling being in lockdown. The minutes, hours, and days get knocked down like a strike in a bowling alley. Most days seem the same. Spring came and went without even giving its consent. Do you realize that it is almost Memorial Day? COVID-19 has robbed us of time, left without a nickel or a dime! I'm ready to get back on track for whatever I have or whatever I lack. Ready to roll? Look for a goal. Hey world, I'm back on track! I've said it before, and I will say it again: Each one of us needs to realize how precious the day is. Sometimes it is fun to do nothing. But now, I realize I am a goal-oriented person who wants to do my best by encouraging others. Each day is an eternal event, never to happen again. Contemplate on it, seize it and live it. The sun is coming through my front window over my neighbor's tree, and the yellow buttercup bush in my garden looks like a bouquet. The day is calling. Ready, set, go - SHINE!!!

May 23rd

I remember a conversation when someone asked me, "Where do you find your happiness?" A simple question for some to answer. I consider myself to be a joyful person, but it was a revelation. Happiness comes in seasons like our lives. I remember being a small boy and believing a two-wheeled bike would bring me immediate delight. As a teenager, getting a car would do the trick. Is there a key to finding happiness so we can open it in bits and pieces that fit the time we live in? Circumstances we have no control over are escalating beyond being difficult. I don't know how to navigate through the turbulence. Still, I am thankful for my ability to see through the fog and expect happiness ahead. I am ever aware of time and the importance in taking baby steps and finding happiness in insignificant pieces and simple places, like seeing a butterfly out in the sunlight or talking with friends in my inner circle. Happiness... not complicated. It does not have strings attached. Even if the feeling darts in like a butterfly, seizes it and lets it take root. And don't forget to water the root with thanksgiving. Find a piece of happiness in your day and Shine!!!

May 24th

Memorial Day: A reflective day - one to remember those who gave their lives for our freedom. I can remember when I was a youth at church, and they spoke the names of the soldiers who died during the Vietnam War. After the service, everyone stepped out into the sunshine to experience everyday life. I can't imagine the pain felt by those families. Then, members from my family left Earth before their time, not from war but from tragic circumstances. I often think about the age they would be now. One grand mystery for me is why some die so young while others live so long. There is no perfect age for death, nor does it seek one. It is a stark reality of life, blended and twisted within the fabric of creation. I will tell you it is my complete trust in GOD Almighty that gives me grains of peace because nothing happens that He does not allow. There must be a plan. When I say "grains" I mean sometimes, like grain, the moments shift through my mind. I experience wonderful days and WHY days. Why does death come at such a youthful age? Telling you   I am always at peace with it would not be the truth. Still, faith wins out, bringing me to my supreme belief that life is a most precious gift. Friends, make the most of time. I tuck away special memories for every one of my loved ones who have gone into eternity in my mind. I bring them out at special moments and smile. Most of you know I work part-time at a grocery store. I'm in the parking lot often.

Whenever I see a dedication to a fallen youth, I say a prayer for them and their family.

Dear God, how great the day will be when every tear gets wiped away and we are reunited with our loved ones! Until then, may our memories fly high and bright. Today, because of these brave men, so does our flag! Shine on Red, White, and Blue!!!

May 26th a.m.

Everyday life day is like a trip to the races. You might win, or you might lose. It's all a gamble! Some people might sit and watch; others jump in and take part. The key word is "moderation." Can anyone tell me if there is a horse named SHINE on the track today? If there is, I plan on placing my bet. Giddy up, gang!!!

May 26th p.m.

Sometimes we sing for those who are mute; other times we dance for those who cannot rejoice. A sweet mix of special talents and gifts. My entire heart sounds that it is our responsibility to use and share our gifts. We may fear, others might ridicule and mock us. But let me tell you, if you can do anything to make someone happy, valued, and whole, then you have found your gift. And buddy, I say use it. One act of kindness, one friendly word, one recognition of someone's worth might change history. Do it, friends. We are pilgrims moving through this 'image' of what we believe life is. This I acknowledge: When we let our love SHINE, it brings us closer to recognizing the purpose of our existence here. For what others may lack, we may possess and vice versa. SHINE with kindness!!!

May 28th a.m.

You know, I think people are beginning to lose their minds. It's an easy thing to do with all kinds of news coming at us from every direction. Dire news spouting out: what you might catch, what could happen, we're all going broke, the world is ending. See my point? Friends, step back, take a deep breath and venture back into the world day by day - a world that never had a guarantee to begin with. Stay with me, please. Quite frankly, I think over the years we started to trust too much on our own resources rather than GOD. If we had the right healthcare program, if we had the correct investments, if we ate the right food. Not that I'm knocking good planning, but somehow GOD was excluded from the portfolio. Man trusted in men...bad idea. I can look no further than my own mistakes. Been-there-done-that. So many times, I never thought of consulting GOD first. Believe me, I paid the cost. Our nation has gone the same route and it has cost us. It does not matter what party you belong to, if GOD is not in the platform, you are in big doo-doo. Faith is needed like never before. Live your life according to RIGHT and WRONG. These are the fundamentals, though not always sought. Shine on with righteousness!!!

May 28th p.m.

Standing in the light of my garden is one of my favorite places to be. It brings me joy, hope and a quiet peace. Sometimes the sunlight shifts, shedding its light in a particular spot, often like our lives. For most of us, life fills our days with both sunshine and rain. Sometimes the shadows fall, and we find ourselves devoid of light. We glance up, waiting for the light to return. The clouds are arranging, moving, and swirling about. We step forward seeking the light, but the clouds block our view. Within my spirit, I hear a soft distant voice that tells me to believe and enclose myself in faith. Keep looking for the light and let your heart soar. Promise exists even in the smallest rays. I know I'll find that place, and you will too if you stand firm and wait until the clouds pass by. Look up and SHINE!!!

May 31st

Opened the front door to the harmonious sounds of LIFE: Birds singing with joy and praises. Brought a new perspective into my day. Are you glued to the television watching the news every morning and night like I am? Troubling events are infiltrating our country in the shroud of darkness. Dear friends, hope still exists; events cannot extinguish it...unless we allow this to happen. We live in a broken world where right and wrong coexist. Strive to work with your fellow man to wipe out the contamination of evil. Together we stand; divided we fall. Put a joyous song in your heart and SHINE ON, SUNDAY!!!

June 1st

Dear friends, this a message I feel I must get out in these most troubling times. Who can deny that our hearts are breaking into a million pieces all over our country? The murder of an innocent man in front of the world - devastating! However, the results of rioting, stealing, destroying and vandalizing were beyond shameful. One thought keeps coming to mind: two wrongs do not make a right. There is no justification in these acts. We must maintain order in a civilized world. I want to guard my heart - a place so intimate and at the core of my being. I will not allow hate to enter inside. But nor will I turn my head and let evil be lauded good and understood. The TEN COMMANDMENTS: I ask every one of you, my friends, to read them again. Maybe it has been a while. I pray for the safety of each of you and your families. Keep LOVE in your heart, but don't sell out to what is politically right either. GOD BLESS AMERICA! SHINE ON!!!

June 3rd

How often have you thought, if only the birds were singing, and the sky was blue? Well today, the birds were singing, and after a rain shower the skies were blue. That's life. I don't know if there ever will be a perfect time. Maybe we should hold on to our happiness and enjoy it as it comes, then take it with us and share it with others, kind of like a picnic lunch. Don't we ALL need nourishment right now? Come on, enjoy the time we have to enjoy. Wishing each one of you a happy Thursday. Open the basket and enjoy the treats! Make this a time that SHINES!!!

June 8th

Many people appear mum about what's going on. I don't think it's out of fear, but most people don't want to offend anyone. Some fear is being labeled racist; others might not care. Maybe it's like talking to someone who has experienced a death in the family. When we say we know how you feel, the truth is we don't. But doesn't the truth often lie somewhere in the middle? Consider what you say and how you say it. When looking at reforms, one needs to be careful about canceling anything. I am not great at debates. After discussions, I wonder why I said what I did. I don't like to argue, even if I may be right. We need to dialog, including the arguments from both sides. Blessed are those who listen. I hope we will. Every life matters...no arguments. To maintain a balanced country, every voice is significant. I want everyone to succeed and have their turn at the bat. A HOME RUN for all of us. SHINE on to Tuesday!!!une 9thWhen I was a young boy, sometimes on Saturday nights our family would go to the local Dairy Queen. My mother loved blizzards; my dad, sister and I usually got dipped cones. Then my father would drive over the bridge to Palm Beach. He'd park the car and my parents would sit on a bench and listen to the waves lap up on the shore. Meanwhile, my sister and I would run up and down the beach. It was magical! The wind would whip through the tall palm trees, and in the distance, we could see the lights of big ships miles away. Sometimes we would walk down the famous "Worth Ave" and like the character, Holly Golightly, we'd window shop because we could not afford to go in. My favorite store was Gucci, which I considered the classiest showing. In my childlike heart I would whisper that one day I'd go in there and shop when my ship came in! Many years later when I had a good paying job, I decided to keep that vintage promise. I drove my Toyota Corolla over the bridge after work with the money from my first paycheck (it was before debit cards; I know, the Stone Age). Bold as brass and still in my postal uniform, I went into the store to buy a new belt. A very polite salesman said to me, "My, that is an interesting costume you have on." High-class manners stopped him from shouting out, "Hey, look at you, straight off the streets!" The important thing is my dream came true! I remembered this when I watched a video of looters in New York stealing from a Gucci store. I am not high- class material, but God bless my parents who taught me to WORK for what I needed and wanted. How very blessed I have been to have parents who taught me the right values. You know what? One of these days I'm heading back for a new belt. Got to earn the dough first, and maybe I'll go all out and get an ice cream cone while I'm at it! "I Scream, You Scream, We all Scream for Ice Cream" (a song written by Howard Johnson, Billy Moll, and Robert A.K. King). SHINE!!!

June 10th

Our world is like a beehive, loud and buzzing, with a flurry of activity going on; you have to be careful, or you might get stung. I feel an undercurrent going on, a hidden force with a definite agenda to cause division. We must be careful before we act. They show us pictures and almost tell us how to react on them. People, we are being set up. Remember the verse I spoke of earlier: The LOVE of many will wax cold. Don't let it happen! The time to be strong is now. You own and maintain the condition of your heart. This force may very well be worse than any virus could ever be! Have a happy Thursday and let your LOVE SHINE BRIGHT!!!

Footnote: Life can be a road trip through many mountains. The secret is to decide which ones to cross over and which ones to avoid. Some prefer gazing from a distance and thinking, how spectacular! Others gas up their vehicles and take off. Beep - Beep!

June 12th

The Story of The Peanut Buttered Mustache: Life can be a humbling experience; embarrassing situations happen. Consider it a lesson in humility. I was a young mailman who ate my lunch in my Jeep. I had just finished part of a route in an upscale clubhouse area. I was eating my usual feast - a simple peanut butter sandwich - when a very attractive lady stopped to talk with me. She was friendly and seemed interested in our conversation. After she left, I smiled. Wow, nice of her to take the time to speak with me. Maybe she thought I was hot to trot! After she walked away, I looked in the mirror and grimaced. To my horror, I had peanut butter plastered all over my mustache! She had been polite - had said nothing about it - yet I felt like a fool. Years later, it's not an enormous deal. Why? Because humble and I are friends. Now I can laugh about it. Me, trying to appear Magnum PI when all the time I looked more like Mr. Turdball. Often, I laugh at myself so much I could cry. Still got the mustache; still love peanut butter. Enjoy the little things in life! SHINE EVERYONE!!!

June 14th

Sunday morning I basked in the sunlight. Touching the grass, talking to my plants, and listening to the sounds of nature always recharges my batteries. Where you find things growing, you will find hope. Can't tell you how many times one of my plants looked like they would die, but sunshine zapped them back to life. Light is one of the most valuable gifts in existence! With it comes hope. I cling to hope, and I look for the light every day. Anything is possible where light exists. Shine, my wonderful friends, SHINE!!!

June 15th

I had the absolute pleasure of being able to say "you are most welcome" after customers thanked me for cleaning the carts at the store. My love for people is a special gift God has given me. When I was younger, someone told to stop being so nice! I can't explain it, but I perceive the good in people. It pains me to say, many perceive the BAD in people first, maybe because of how someone looks, or where they come from, and often for what they stand for. Statisticians strive to point out the percentage of people who are bad or worthless. Well, I can't deny evil people exist. But if we seek altruistic people, these numbers will minimize the bad. I believe a multitude of kindhearted people exist in the world! We need to expect good, reflect good and show goodwill with our actions. SHINING by example - how outstanding is that?

June 16th

ONE of our greatest issues is the power of "The Thought Police," people with powerful agendas grasping to control the masses by brainwashing them. It's called marketing and advertising, not only for products, but by making the masses their products! How many people hand over their power to someone who tells them how to dress, wear their hair (for those lucky enough to have some) or what food they should eat? One of our greatest gifts is free will, the capacity to choose without being influenced by others. We are free to choose our behavior, yet I see so many people rushing into the mob mentality. They are doing it, so it must be right. Want to teach the young a great, lifelong gift and ability? Teach them to judge for themselves! Don't become a pawn or instrument for anyone's agenda. Guard your mind and listen to your inner voice. Be still and you will feel your light Shine!!!

Footnote: IF YOU HAVE TO "WORK" AT BEING WHO YOU REALLY ARE, THEN YOU ARE IN THE WRONG PROFESSION!

June 17th

This morning, a friend and I were discussing the condition the world is in. Need I say more? I think many people have ideas on what might be needed. But this song awakened my weary heart, a song I once sang in church: "Let there be peace on earth and let it begin with me." Most of us possess little power over anything. What we have within our own being is the power to show love to everyone. Did you know that you could be a superhero? Someone who is kind, thoughtful and treats everyone you meet with the respect that you, yourself, would like to have. It's really simple. One person at a time can make a difference. The Bible says, "Blessed are the peacemakers, for they shall be called sons of God." Are you willing to go the extra mile?

Sending out love to all the superheroes in the world. Keep on SHINING by example!!!

June 17th

I steered clear of the news this week. My opinion is that we are being set up as an earthquake vibrates across our land. One story after the other, some ludicrous! I can't become an ostrich and hide my head in the sand. I would rather seek a calming place to sort through my thoughts. I am firm on my beliefs, but I don't feel the need to carry a sign or beat a drum. I'd rather live by my words and with like-minded actions. Friends, I would be stupid not to see storm clouds brewing in the distance and carry on unprepared. Know who you are and stand firm. I remember one time during a storm, a ray of light streaked through the darkness with a message of hope. May each of us endure the darkness in search of the light. SHINE on through the storms of life as our courage propels us forward.

June 18th

Have you ever had angels in YOUR outfield? In all of our lives, at certain times, there have been angels present to help us - some heavenly and some earthly. I was a young, newbie letter carrier and I went to a hilly neighborhood to deliver mail. Our early training prepared us to put safety first. Engine off, brake on, key in hand. Well, I parked on a hill going down into a busy highway. I DID all those things instructed except I did not pull the brake up tight. I walked up to a house and an older black woman came out the door. "Honey, your Jeep is rolling!" she cried. I ran like a deer and stopped it. This sweet angel saved my life, my career, and my future. I never saw her again. And she doesn't know it, but she lives on in my heart. One day, God might give you a chance to be an angel. So be ready in the outfield. You might be up to bat, hit a home run and score one for humanity! Shine, my angels, SHINE!!!

June 21st

At work, I watch people stand in line to buy lotto tickets and I wish them good luck! But if you can walk, talk, eat, sleep and enjoy life, you have won the lottery already. Yeah, piles of money come in handy and make life easier. Truth is…I don't need more to make me happy. There are still some big-ticket dream wishes on my list. If I get them, that's great; if I don't get them, that's great too. Like the famous song goes, "You can't always get what you want. But if you try sometimes, you find you get what you need." I am trying *soooo* hard not to be a needy person. Sometimes we set ourselves up for trouble when we feel that we deserve more. So count your blessings and you've got a winning TICKET. Now on to my next blessing. A new day awaits. You are a winner. SHINE on Monday!!!

June 22nd

Dearest friends: Don't let your hearts become hardened by the division out there. Many people seem angry and filled with hate. Many people are kind and desire to live in peace. The media appear as a big ugly monster, ready to fill your minds with fear and anxiety. I have turned off the major news stations. Instead, I'm listening to my favorite music stations and grounding myself in my favorite places to be - in the garden and here with you! I love to view your posts on social media. Pictures with your families help me discover a little about you; I like that. Hope springs forth and I believe that life will go on to good places. What I write here is important to me. When we feel healthy and find interesting things to do, we are a blessed people. For those of you younger, I can only tell you how fast life goes. Life is like a RED sports car, so drive it for all it's worth! Blue, yellow or whatever color you like will work, too. Live your life to the fullest. The worst thing about wearing a mask is my smile: no one can see it. Despite all the dissension, I am finding a lot to smile about these days, like having friends like you! Spread love, happiness and much needed hope into the universe. Rev up your engines and Shine!!!

June 25th

Some days are like buying an old, tired car, but you GET IN AND DRIVE IT ANYWAY! A story for you: When my dad was young, money was tight, and he needed a new car. The salesman assessed the amount of dollars in Dad's wallet and showed him a weather-beaten old heap. Dad gulped when the salesman told him the mileage on the car; someone had driven it to the moon and back. The salty old salesman told Dad to "Get your ass in the car and take it for a spin!" The car drove like a champ and turned out to be one of the best cars my dad ever had. Well, today might look weather-beaten but get your derriere in this day and drive it for all it's worth. Who knows, it might be one of the best days in your life. Honk, honk. SHINE!!!

June 29th

Heat wave alert! The weather can seep into your day and make you feel miserable. It makes me wonder about the people who display a table of contents to a book of how very difficult life is today. These people don't have a clue. My grandfather and his father and those before them came from a long line of farmers. Not the big successful ones, but the ones who worked the land to put food on their tables. During the Depression, can you imagine working all day and then going inside a home without air conditioning, an indoor bathroom and other things that this blessed generation has? I will be frank about a lot of wimps out here crying the blues who do not understand. Even the middle class possess so many things our families never had. And why are people tearing down statues? My response: DO YOUR HOMEWORK. Put your energy into something constructive! We might be at the most convenient point in history to live. Thank those who came before us. I worked at my part-time job today and when I got home, I proceeded out into the heat to mow the lawn. Afterwards, I reached into my cool fridge to get a cool drink and sat down inside my cool house. I thought about my ancestors who came before me and I raised my glass for a toast - good JOB! Life is challenging but also wonderful. My weather forecast for Tuesday is it's going to be a fantastic day to SHINE!!!

July 2nd

GOD has impeccable eyesight; He sees what we cannot. It is difficult to understand why HE uses those we deem unworthy. Thus, a prayer: Dear GOD, help us see the good in each other so the work that you have prepared for each of us may fulfill Your plan. Amen. SHINE in God's amazing graces!!!

July 4th

The Rites to Happiness: Have you ever heard the saying he (or she) was born happy? Well, I think I was, even though - when at three months old - I contracted spinal meningitis and almost died. My mother and her friends prayed for my recovery, and God answered those prayers - perhaps because He had other plans for me. In life, I seek happiness. I even sought happiness through the difficult bullying school years. What I often ponder is, is it within us or do we gain it by merit? Having worked most of my adult life with the public, I've seen it all - from the most delightful, interesting people, to some who could make a train stop in its tracks and want to turn around. There have been situations in my way of life that threatened to swallow me up like a giant tidal wave. I was sure that these situations conspired to wash away any trace of happiness within me. And the question that follows asks, "Do we deserve happiness?" Heck yes! WE ALL DESERVE TO BE HAPPY! So I am shifting the question. Yes, you can be born with a certain disposition. But happiness is also a choice. So what are the most important traits to incorporate in order to be happy? Show gratitude, focus on the present, laugh often, and demonstrate self- confidence. Adapt to situations that come your way; being optimistic should be high on your list. I had a young boy on one of my mail routes who was mentally challenged and also had physical restrictions. Despite everything, he was such a joyous, happy person, and his million-dollar smile lit up the world. I always looked forward to seeing him. He exemplified the rite to happiness, right smack down to the very core. And so can we. Friends - choose happiness. Shine and have a blessed Fourth!!!

July 6th

Give me the honor of naming a mountain, and I would choose the name Good Intentions. Why? That is how I perceive my life. On top of the world, excited to begin each day with good intentions. But most times these positive thoughts go downhill. It's easy to shift the blame on situations or other people. Is it caused by living in a complex world with complex situations? I believe it's all in how we handle it. Don't let yourself go into detention because you had good intentions. The secret is to stay on course with your original plan. Practice good intentions! Not always easy. I am in the classroom learning too. I want to stay on my mountain where the view is outstanding, the air is clean, and where I can SHINE with good intentions. Time to move on to this mountainous Monday. SHINE!!!

July 7th

Dear friends, quite a few people believe that COVID-19 is a hoax.

How can this be true? So many people have died! Young, old, weak, strong... the virus has no boundaries. Scientists are striving to unlock the mysteries like why some people are carriers and others show little to no symptoms, and how most become sick but suffer no lasting ill effects. And in the worst-case scenarios, many individuals who are hospitalized suffer a myriad of problems: strokes, amputations, and difficulty breathing on their own. One brave wife fought the battle for her husband at home while his body endured devastating consequences in the ICU. She refused to give up, in sickness and in health. Virus-free, but still hanging on in the hospital; there was a heartbreaking picture of the couple clasping hands on social media. He did not make it. This wonderful man in the prime of his life died, leaving his wife and toddler son to carry on in these troubling times. His legacy: Live your Life to the fullest. This angel is in Heaven; his soul mate continues to live life on earth with conviction and hope! God bless her. Like a true warrior, she SHINES on for both of them!!!

July 8th

In the mid-60's, one of my favorite TV shows was "Green Acres."
Two of my favorite characters happened to be a brother and sister
blundering carpenter team called the Monroe Brothers. They
were forever working on repairing the bedroom in a broken-down
farmhouse. As a boy, my father told me about a real-life builder
(during the Depression) and how his homes were quirky and
rather off-keel. When my father drove by one, he'd say, "that's
one of the so-and-so homes." Well, I kind of liked them because
they were unique - one of a kind. Growing up, I was a "Monroe
Brother." My handyman skills are quirky and off-keel - original and
never perfect. I've had friends who are skilled perfectionists, and
I admire their precise and well-thought-out finished products.
Perhaps many of us try to start out with perfect blueprints, but
then (remember this is an imperfect world we live in), flaws
materialize everywhere. Even plants can be quirky. I have a line of
cypress trees that I planted at the same time. Most of them grew
tall, but one of them is smaller, grew tilted, and refuses to get with
the program. I bet it will become the best looking of the bunch.
Flaws can drive us crazy, but still, it's the flaws we remember.
Should we strive for perfection? Yes. Practice patience with the
imperfect people in your world. After all, aren't you one of them?
Hey, look at me! STILL not perfect, but a work in progress. Now
where did I put my carpenter's level? SHINE ON, SHINERS!!!

Footnote: "Green Acres" was a quirky sitcom about a lawyer and his socialite wife who moved from New York to a broken-down farmhouse out in the country. It starred Eddie Albert and Eva Gabor. Alf (Sid Melton) and his "brother" Ralph (Mary Grace Canfield) were the quarrelsome carpenters on the show.

July 12th

Dear Friends: Many times in my life, I wanted to be someone else - better, smarter, stronger, popular, or someone from a wealthy background. I could go on. Has anyone else felt that way? In school, it was easy to pick out the winners, students who accomplished all that and better - appearing at the right time and place. Now, in our society, there seems to be a "push" to push everyone to the front of the class. Now here I go again; stick with me. Perhaps we are who we are right smack dab to serve a purpose. If we show patience and hold steady, sometimes we can grasp a glimpse of why. One red flag for me to acknowledge... If only I had been "all that." As I look back, my classroom helped me to understand what it takes to overcome. Because I overcame, I can empathize and try to help others. Yes, we need the hills in our lives, but we also need valleys if we are to learn. This has become an instant generation... give it to us now. Well, I'm sixty-four and still climbing the mountain. I earned it one step at a time, and to my amazement, right now I can say I like the man in the mirror. After a tough journey, life fits me like a glove now. Love the person you are and love your neighbor as yourself! HAPPY SUNDAY. SHINE!!!

July 17th

Rejoice in what there is, NOT in what is not your life. My parents gave my older sister a lot of responsibility with her younger siblings. I remember her making us dinner with leftovers and turning them into a gourmet meal. If there were old curtains around, she would make new curtains and turn the window into a showcase. After she got her first job, on a shoe-string budget she put two jackets on layaway for my sister and I to wear to school. I suppose so many of us would love it if everything we needed was right on the shelf or if we had a stockpile of money lying around, but I believe talent exists in finding what you needed all along - right in front of your face - making it happen on your own merit and hard work. The key word is hard work, and the merits you have in knowing that you accomplished it all by yourself. SHINE!!!

July 19th

I love Sundays because they are my days of reflection. I put all my ambitions (many) in a trunk. Then I slide into neutral. For me, it's like breathing space for the week to come; a day designated as a free space. Diets not allowed. I can eat my candy bar, what the heck. I sit out on my front porch, daydream and note how much the grass has grown. GOD knew what he was doing, giving us this day to rest. Even the cats agree. They lie down by the dining room window, bird watching and snoozing here and there. Why not? Friends, there may be mountains you need to climb this week so sit back and enjoy the view. Aw, I am enjoying this peaceful day and taking the time to SHINE!!!

July 21st

There's talk about a coin shortage going on. This brings back wonderful memories because I remember how much a DIME would buy you when I was a kid! My sister and I used to look under the cushions of our old couch hoping to hit pay dirt. Sometimes my aunt would let us shake out her old purses and collect all the change that fell out. In those days, some of you might remember the Farm and Dairy Store. It was a drive thru store that had sliding glass doors on each side. Talk about modern conveniences! We had one up the road from our house. With a DIME you could buy an ice cream sandwich or a small bag of chips! Or you might ride your bike across the street to a bakery store and buy day old pastries. Man, with a quarter and five dimes you felt rich. Funny how inexpensive treats were back then. There is an old saying, "A penny for your thoughts." These days, you pull out your credit or debit card. Hey, going to count some change. Thinking about buying an ice cream sandwich. Pennies, nickels and dimes, boy do they SHINE!!!

July 23rd

The day you feel sorry for yourself, you are a dead duck!
Everyone on the face of this earth has pluses and minuses, and
that's the stark truth. I just don't see any good coming out of the
"poor me" syndrome. Many of my personal heroes had a lot of
zeros, but whatever they did was "working" for them. I first met
[I'll call him] "Arnie" when I started working as a letter carrier.
Arnie had lost both his legs and got around in his wheelchair. I
never asked what happened. He never said. He was one hard-
nosed character who talked like a truck driver and had a heart of
gold. He could maneuver that chair like a driver in the Indy 500.
At the time I met him, his wife required care because of an illness,
and Arnie became her caretaker. Not once did he complain to me
except to say he'd seen better times. He added, "But what the
hell!" Look, I understand things can be tough now that I'm
approaching the senior years. You rehearse the aches and the
pains. Time will not let you escape. But I go at it with vim and
vigor, striving to be the best I can be without bellyaching. Every
time Arnie comes to mind, I can hear this precious man barking in
my head, "You gotta be tough, kid; you gotta be tough!" Thank
you, God, for all You have given me. Somewhere, some place,
Arnie must know I'm thinking about him, and I hope he is smiling
because I am. May every one of you Shine as bright as Arnie did!!!

July 26th

One of the worst side effects of this deadly virus is the distance it has created between us and the power of human touch. When we receive a hug, this simple tactile sensation reassures us someone cares. It seeps into the soul as energy and speeds up the healing process of body, mind, and spirit. This energy of love has endured every calamity and disaster brought upon humanity throughout the ages. The touch of LOVE is perhaps the greatest form of validation ever received. Don't you cherish sweet memories of loved ones who have passed on? Doesn't their caring touch live on in your hearts? Yes, we must follow the advice and instructions given if we are to survive. I am looking forward to the day when I will receive and give a hug. We must create a hug symbol and here is mine to you. Have a blessed Sunday as I reach out to you with a great big virtual HUG. :D< SHINE!!!

July 27th

The old family recliner chair in my house has seen better days.

When I sit down, it is so comfortable that I can fall asleep at the drop of a hat. And so it goes with our lives. Who doesn't want an easy life? But then again, we might fall asleep and miss the program. This happens to me often. Nothing wrong with an uncomplicated life. But I can also tell you it was, in so many cases, the hard places that led me to believe and have faith. Difficult times also provided me with the skills I needed to survive. Years ago, I had a customer - an older woman - who was the sweetest soul I had ever met! On her front door was a card that read, Don't pray for a calm life, pray for the strength to endure a difficult one. To be honest, I didn't value the meaning of it at that time. I wanted everything to be easy. But doesn't a catch or clause get added into the contract? And I hear my late, dear father's voice, "Life is not meant to be easy." Every day, friends, we must give it our best shot. Look for the best; expect the best. But also pray that we can endure an earthly life. Crude, but true, you- know- what can hit the fan. So make this a glorious day. Ease on down the road and watch out for potholes. Tonight I will sit in my comfortable recliner as I contemplate the events of the day. Someone please wake me up if I fall asleep. Shine!!!

July 28th

"The Eyes of Fear." I work with the public. Therefore, the opportunity exists to gaze into the eyes of the soul. I miss the smiles, but now it's all about the "eyes." And like a machine that records emotions and feelings with a needle that shows the range, I will tell you about my insightful observations. Sometimes in the eyes, I see fear and the needle points toward the "panic'' mode. Other times the monitor is in the middle showing survival mode. It's a rare occurrence when the needle points to "nothing here to worry about." Where are you on the monitor? I'd say my needle is pointing to the concerned range. There is a responsibility to do everything possible to obey the rules, so I respect everyone I come in contact with. I do not enjoy wearing a mask. Still, it's the right thing to do. I met a man who said it was all a rube, and we have become like "sheep." Likewise, I've met people stuck in the fear mode big-time. I understand. These are strange days. I long for the day when the needle reads NORMAL! Some say it never will. I beg to differ. Then I will frame my mask as a constant reminder of these days and how fortunate we are that this time has passed. Then our eyes can move from fear to sheer joy and thanksgiving. I believe that day is coming. Keep hoping, moving forward and keep Shining!!!

Footnote: There's hope on the horizon!!! A vaccine for the virus is in its critical third phase - epic news. A possibility of a vaccine by the end of the year?

PART 11

Once upon a time, in the mystical village of Kytirus, a dreaded virus spread throughout the kingdom. All the creatures living near the river became paralyzed with fear. "What can we do? Where can we hide?" they asked with a quiver. An answer came from the enlightened one, Kroll, who tugged on his long white beard and proclaimed everyone should stay inside! So, for many days, the creatures obeyed Kroll's order. It was so lonely that sometimes they cried. Oh, if only they could go outside, frolicking in the sunshine, forgetting about this awful time. Mother mouse, within her house, brought forth an idea. As head of the family, it was her task. She held up an object fashioned out of cloth. "Why doesn't everyone wear a mask?" She looked around at their startled faces. "And when you play with some resistance, keep a safe and happy distance!" Her son, the little mouse, ventured from the house. He played on the river's bank and ran fast up the hills, but he always had on his little mask. The other creatures gawked at the sight of a mouse wearing a mask. "Doesn't he look silly?" they laughed. He should have stayed in bed and covered his head! Then Percival, the wise old owl who spoke with a persnickety growl, scolded the others. "Nonsense, fools. He's got the right idea. It's a special tool that will keep us safe while we try to live in this horrible place." After he spoke, the parents lectured their children with a firm poke. "Now everyone, young and old, here are some masks designed for you." All the mice continued with this trend, and that's how it all began. And soon the virus disappeared. Yeah, the mask restored peace to Kytirus. Sometimes even a simple creature has invaluable words of wisdom! Good things come forth with no surprise. If we do the right thing; we'll be back on track. Keep your chin up and maintain a smile under your mask. Better days are coming, Shine on!!!

July 29th

Kindness always wins. I stand by this statement. Yesterday, from the top ranks of government, I observed a group of so-called intelligent people acting like rude, spoiled children. So difficult to understand. Don't act foolish because you believe that only your opinions matter. Acting and behaving in a mean-spirited way is unacceptable under any circumstances. Because then you have lost the argument. My parents showed everyone respect and expected the same from their children. Are we losing that quality as a nation? If we are, then it's a sad day. I love Aretha Franklin's music, and my favorite song is R-E-S-P-E-C-T. I know what it means to me; how about you? Show the world your best side. Whoa, baby time to SHINE!!!

Footnote: Kindness is the language that the deaf can hear and the blind can see. - Mark Twain.

July 30th

Have you ever told someone about a wish you have only to be shot down with, "Stop dreaming; it's not going to happen." Everyone needs a dream…one we can nurture and keep alive. Dreams do not have expiration dates. I read that a man in his nineties was graduating from college. Yes, hard work dwells in the mix. But isn't anything possible? So follow that dream, even if obstacles try to block the path. Not all paths lead to roses and daffodils. Heck, mine has cactus and rocks scattered here and there. Evaluating the footpath ahead is a good start. Friends, don't be afraid to embrace your dreams; they can steer you towards everyday life with a spring in your step. Keep them safe; take extraordinary care of them because they… belong… to…you! Sprinkle your day with unlimited opportunities. May all your dreams SHINE on!!!

Footnote: Some stay in bed and dream; others dare to go out and live them. During my younger years, fear tried to keep me captive. In my prime, I could still do the time, but many clouds were cluttering my mind. Now it's a task since I have to wear a mask. At long last, I'm living out large. Some gifts come late. But "better late than never." FRIENDS, despite where you are in life, open your gifts and let your colors SHINE!!!

August 2nd

This continues to be a bizarre year. News flash: Experts may advise people to wear masks in their homes. WHAT? I draw the line here. No, nada, out of the question! Sometimes I have to wear a mask for hours. It makes me feel like there's sawdust in my throat. UGH, even I go through my rebellious moments. Get a good night's rest before moving on to Monday. Shining off… chow, baby!!!

August 4th

Life is very unpredictable. A few days ago there was a dread of an approaching hurricane, but it turned into only a spattering of rain. Today, tremendous amounts of rain pelted our parking lot at work. I had to drive through some flooded areas to get home. Such are our days here on earth: uncertain with no promises guaranteed. Many times at the end of a day, I search inside my soul, like a shopkeeper sizing up his merchandise. Have I been courageous, respectful, honest, forgiving and kind, or did I leave them on the shelf not putting them to good use? Yes, there is plenty of room for improvement. Isn't that good news? If everyone desired to be thoughtful, respectful, and more caring, what a difference that could make! Tomorrow is only hours away. So here's the chance to do your part. Open up your stockroom and analyze your wares. Today it was my honor to serve others with dedication and respect.

My stock room was emptied, and my shelves have extra room for tomorrow's inventory. It's from the greatest supplier of all. May God's blessing be upon you. Shine on to Wednesday with a stock room full of abundance!!!

August 5th

I chatted with my younger neighbors, children who are planning to return to school. Nothing is set in stone yet, and fear and frustrations rule. Will they go back to school or will their parents opt for online learning? The school system is struggling to develop a safe plan for 50 million students. So sad. I remember being excited at the start of a new school year. A trip to the store to pick out school gear was always fun. School supplies like book bags, pencils, paper and crayons each carried a distinct scent of newness. Once we arrived and the school bell rang, we were excited to find out who our teachers and friends would be. But now unique challenges complicate once normal situations like riding the bus, eating in the cafeteria, and gym class. I can't imagine how students and teachers will deal with wearing masks and social distancing. God bless them! With all honesty, friends, I am glad my children are all grown. This will be a toughie. These children are the future; I wish the best for them. Wow, a lot has changed since 1962 when I shuffled to my first school desk with my Deputy Dawg lunch box. The Beverly Hillbillies were airing on television and the new dance step was the TWIST. My first-grade teacher was a lovely nun named Sister Margaret Mary. I called her Sister Madagascar. She disappeared around Christmas and supposedly returned to her home convent for an extended rest...I had nothing to do with it! SHINE ON to a tolerant THURSDAY!!!

August 7th a.m.

Mere mortals are egotistical creatures placing importance on themselves. Consider this: We are a grain in the sand, a pebble on the beach of LIFE. Live with humbleness. Appreciate your time on the stage. The curtain closes on the last act before you know it. Somewhere, someplace, a small new star is traveling into the earthly light, a new life to carry the torch and possibly shine brighter than those who came before. Sometimes a small child or baby comes through the line at my workplace and our eyes meet with curiosity. For me, it's awesome because I see wisdom in the innocent eyes of a child. I wonder what the child sees in my eyes. In my heart and spirit I attempt to pass on positive vibes: "Good luck, little one, for you are the future!" God bless all the newborn babies. May they abide in his love and SHINE in his light!!!

August 7th p.m.

This is the WORST of times; this is the BEST of times. From a famous book? I have an agenda to send light into the world during this period of darkness. LIGHT and light alone can be such an extraordinary entity. When we punch out on our final time clock, all titles and possessions will count for nothing. What will count is how we lived our lives. Did we put God first and did we love our neighbor as ourselves? Many feel afraid and angry in this upside-down world right now. Remember that kindness can lighten a heavy heart. Be that light, for light dispels darkness. Reach out for your chance to transform someone's existence. Wake up tomorrow with joy in your heart. SHINE your light in the darkness and I will Shine mine!!!

Footnote: "Remember, when you leave this earth you can take with you nothing that you have received, only what you have given. A heart enriched by honest service, love, sacrifice and courage." -Saint Francis of Assisi.

August 9th

Have you gone to a movie and then walked out before it ended?

Kind of like our situation today. There are times we can't keep watching! Friends, don't walk out! We will make it to the credits. And the credits depend on you! Faith, good behavior, and perseverance will pick you up by the bootstraps and propel you forward. We did not write this story, but we can write our own part in the script. My script reads: The man behind this mask is STILL smiling. No matter how far the distance. I plan on persevering until we reach a happy ending. Yes, living thru the pandemic is mind blowing. But if you latch onto God's graces, you will be able to endure the days to come. No walking out for me. I'll see this to the end. Please don't give up; let your Sunday SHINE with determination!!! "Don't be afraid to SHINE. There is always someone who needs your light." – Ziglar.com

August 10th

Today, an age-old question for you: If you found a bottle with a magic genie inside and he granted you three wishes, what would you ask for? I am sure most everyone's first wish would be for this virus to disappear. Mine is. My second wish is that the U.S. economy will bounce back and surpass where we left off before the pandemic. My third wish would be for an easy, stress-free life. Ok…I am not being heartfelt about my third choice because I actually wish that my infant son, who died many years ago, would be alive and well today. But here it comes…a perfect life does not exist. Most of you have family and friends you'd love to be with again. And who doesn't want sickness eradicated on earth? No question when it involves children! Sometimes I wish I could change HISTORY, but that wish alone might alter the true purpose of our lives here. OK, my wishes ran out a long time ago. The list goes on and on. Friends, I realize how amazing our lives would be if only every wish we wish would come true. I'm banking on that happening in a perfect place - a most magnificent place where every wish comes true. Perhaps some might say all their wishes have come true. Bravo for them; I've yet to find that bottle. Stay safe, productive, and kind on this magical Monday. Tonight my wish upon a star will be that HOPE SHINES ON!!!

August 12th

This is one of the toughest seasons I've dealt with in ages. The virus, politics, fear, and not to mention layers and layers of attitude! I've had many jobs in my season of life. One was sanding down cars to get prepped for a new paint job. I remember many already had layers after layers of old paint jobs. These cars required a great deal of attention. How about you; how many layers do you have? Somewhere beneath the mask we wear, the authentic "person" lives. The secret is to nurture it and keep it going. Like sandpaper grit, life's circumstances can be rough. The undercurrents surface in many; I hear, see and understand it. But don't let it consume the 'true' you. This season WILL pass. Be a wonderful genuine person in the arena of life and your patina will glow. Have a superpower Wednesday, Masked Marvels, and let your finish SHINE!!!

August 13th

Allow people to think for themselves, and most will choose to live in harmony and peace. The problem arises when individuals promote discord and anarchy in the world for selfish reasons. Their agenda is bent on pulling people apart. When chaos erupts, people look for easy solutions. We live in a time where simple answers do not exist. The knowledge mankind has acquired has grown to phenomenal heights. So why leave GOD out of the equation when He has given us His greatest gift…life? Friends, we need to revisit those thoughts. No man or woman alone can lead us to victory. It's not what the party can do for you, it's the person you portray outside of the party. We will not find our answers in flesh and blood men, rather in GOD ALMIGHTY. Keep SHINING!!!

Footnote: Russia recently approved the world's first vaccine for COVID-19 but reports that clinical trials have not been completed. Scientists denounce the certification as premature. The Russian president endorsed "Sputnic V" and said it had passed all the necessary steps. Little details were given about the vaccine except that a phase three trial will began on August 12th in Russia.

August 13th

Had some interesting dreams last night. Sometimes I remember them, sometimes I don't. But today, I want to talk about the mechanism of "day-dreaming." I think it's important to indulge ourselves with pleasant thoughts throughout the day. One of my favorite things to do late afternoons is sit out on my front porch and look out at the lawn, bushes, and flowers, and daydream. Lately, a small rabbit hops out to lie on the lawn and visit. Yesterday we checked each other out. It was a sweltering day, so I placed some "goodies" on the lawn and filled a flat container with fresh water. While I'm outside watching nature, I envision visiting Cotswold in England and admiring their charming gardens. Sometimes I recall my vacations in the picturesque Great Smoky Mountains, a place dear to my heart. And while I'm out there, a beautiful butterfly makes the rounds and small lizards are leaping everywhere in constant movement. Nature - the nature of life - and just letting my mind relax. We work our minds to the point of exhaustion sometimes. Perhaps we need a reminder to give our brains a rest. Does anyone remember this song? "What a day for a daydream. What a day for a daydreaming boy." Take care, friends. Rest here and there during the day. And don't forget to keep your dreams close to your heart where they will SHINE!!!

August 14th

Sometimes a voice in my head calls me to action. Have you had an intuitive moment like this? Many months ago, I felt the urge to connect with a friend from the past. I can't say enough about her compassionate nature. She was a loyal friend who would drop everything to come help you. We moved away; her family moved away. Time slipped in between us. I don't know why, but a voice told me to make my appreciation known to the super-stars who enlightened my life. One day, I phoned her and made this happen. A couple weeks ago, her husband and I were in contact and he told me that his wife was ill from an unforeseen condition. Yesterday, I found out she died while in the hospital. She leaves behind a husband, daughter, grandchildren, parents and brothers...and also a friend who will keep her memory within his heart. I was so blessed to have this precious woman in my life! It is a mystery why some people live long lives and others do not. That is why I practice gratitude every day and strive to "get it right." Use your time well. Goodbye, sweet friend, for death has called your name and I must carry on. Friends, grasp onto the golden ring called LIFE and SHINE!!!

Footnote: If only death could take a holiday! There was a 1934 movie about this concept and a remake in 1971. One of the most difficult and horrendous things about this pandemic is when family members and friends cannot visit a loved one who is in the hospital...especially when the patient's condition is life-threatening. Many times, hospital staff are holding their patient's hand as they take their last breath. There are five stages of grief: denial, anger, bargaining, depression, and acceptance. But imagine the shock of dropping a loved one off at the hospital and then never seeing them again! Please, Covid...Go Away!!!

August 15th

Often, we desire to be something we are not. Maybe one wants to be more attractive, smarter or famous. WE forget about the person inside. But it is the PERSON INSIDE that God created us to be. When we realize and act upon it, so comes the gift. Sometimes - many times - it's not what we see that brings greatness, rather what we believe in. Do the world a favor: grasp who you are. Be yourself and SHINE with genuineness!!!

August 17th

I wonder if it is much easier for us to find something to be mad or upset about rather than being happy. We are living in a place that sometimes lends itself to catastrophe. Does anyone recall those simple cartoon images that read "Happiness is?" I do. Right now, wouldn't you agree that happiness is a Covid-free world? Many of us are children of the television era where we were spoon fed the recipe for happiness. But isn't the recipe different for everyone?

I'll never forget a homeless man in my neck of the woods who rode a bike with a homemade trailer on the back. He adorned it with an American flag, and it was filled with his belongings. His scruffy dog had an old rope for a leash and sometimes rode in the trailer. Both of them looked so content. Believe me, it would not be my wish, but by golly it was a statement! The perfect recipe is to have a happy heart. Follow your destination to a day filled with peace and tranquility. Happiness is letting your light Shine and aspiring others to Shine along with you!!!

Footnote: Charlie Chaplin was 88 years old when he left this earth. He died on 12/25/77 in Switzerland. A British actor, known for his work in Silent Films, he was also a movie maker, screenwriter, and author. Some of his quotes included:

-You will never find a rainbow if you are looking down.

-A day without laughter is a day wasted.

-*Imagination means nothing without doing.*

-*Life is just a journey! Therefore, live today!*

You rock, Charlie Chaplin!!!

August 19th

Perhaps it is my age, but I've been around the block of life many, many times. I can now say I do not feel the necessity for apprehension. Once, things seemed like life or death. Now life is life and death is death. I am trying to enjoy the show, this thing called LIFE. What do you think? Let's have some fun and allow the story to unfold. There are many things we cannot control. Yes, we need to pay attention and keep our eyes wide open, but don't let the story overpower you. I gazed out at my beautiful garden and the tranquility of the day soothed my soul. Claim those times and relish them, far from the noise and the crowds. Medicine for the soul. Blessings for a peaceful Thursday. Take time and allow yourself some well-earned reflective moments, you deserve them. SHINE ON SHINERS!!!

Footnote: "Take my yoke upon you, and learn from me, for I am gentle and lowly in heart, and you will find rest for your soul." Matthew 11:29.

August 25th

A mask might cover your mouth these days, but do not allow one to cover your heart. Love everyone around you, and no virus, evil or fear can survive, for LOVE is the most powerful force God has given us. When we love each other, we are proclaiming the majesty of our Creator. All good things come from GOD! With God in our hearts, fear does not exist. Is this the worst of times? Perhaps, but we must not allow the circumstances to bring the worst out in us. Let the BEST of you encourage everyone you meet. This devastating time will not last forever. With LOVE in our hearts, we will bring forth the BEST. Wishing YOU, my friends, only the best. SHINE forth!!!

The older I become, the more aware I am about colors. I love bright colors because of their pizzazz. If you were to search my closet, you'd find the dominate color is yellow. To me, it's a happy, bright reflective color. Just call me yellow mellow. Today, I am planning for a bright, colorful, outstanding day. I guess some might say it's a roll of the dice, kid! But I am holding my expectations high. My job requires me to wear green, so I'll be wearing green. Unseen and deep inside of my soul YELLOW is on the roll. Friends, seize the day. Shine and color your world with inspiration!!!

August 28th

I enjoy eating a hard-boiled egg, hands down. The simplicity of an egg: easy to eat, packed with protein, and in a fast lifestyle on the run, a winning snack. After you "crack" the shell, victory! Some of us have been like hard-boiled eggs in our lives. Tough shells on the outside, soft on the inside, trying to protect the vulnerability of who we are. Some people are ostracized for being different. What a shame! Especially when the criticism comes close to home. Well, it's taken me a lifetime to recognize the value in the uniqueness of a person. How wonderful diversity is. Some have accused me of liking weird people. Strange, because I think they are unique creations. Honest fascinating beings daring to be who they are. And put me on that list. I've come to the place where I'm happy being me. What about you? Out of your shell and feeling well. You are one of a kind and ready to shine, no apologies necessary. Embrace respect for your fellow man with an open heart. And yes, it's alright and good to love who you are. So 'egg on' everyone to Shine!!!

Footnote: "Look at how a single candle can both defy and define the darkness." -Anne Frank

August 28th

What is your state of mind today? Have you become complacent with politics and the unrest that is bent on dividing our great nation? Not to mention living in a virus filled world where you wear a mask, social distance, and limit your activities. Yes, the virus rages on amid violence and social injustice. Like Rip Van Winkle, we've been asleep too long. There was nuclear blast in our backyard. Brace yourself, the dust is still settling in. You close your windows, lock your doors, and then you get used to it. No - open your windows, unlock your doors and do something about it. Dear friends, wake up before it is too late. God is slow to anger, but He sees the hate, destruction and division. We are under judgment…God's judgment. Please listen and think about this. Strive to build faith for a new tomorrow. Pray we can emerge as one nation under God with liberty and justice for all! Otherwise we will never STAND together. All good things come from God. Wake up, America, and Shine!!!

Footnote: I know that some of you may feel helpless because of everything that is going on in the world. "What can I do," you might ask? If you want to develop a deeper relationship with God quiet your minds, open your hearts and allow the Holy Spirit to guide your thoughts. In the Bible, Jesus told His disciples a parable to show them that they should always pray for just causes and never give up. You may want to read the Parable of the Unjust Judge as food for thought.

August 30th

Given politics, news, and this dreaded virus, I've been struggling to decipher the history of mankind. Man keeps making mistakes by choosing not to follow the rules. Remember being little and asking our parents if we could go out in the backyard and play? The answer was usually yes. But they added, "Do not play in the street!" If we disobeyed our parents, they paddled our derrieres, and it stopped us from doing it again. It keeps coming back to: People don't want to follow the rules. Take The Ten Commandments, for example. You need not be Einstein to interpret what they mean. Ever since the Garden of Eden, mankind has rebelled. Friends, has society reached a place where many feel they do not need GOD to fix our problems? The political parties are saying, WE CAN FIX THE PROBLEMS if you VOTE for us! I'm sure if I went up on stage reading "The Ten Commandments" a tomato or two would come flying out to hit me in the face. I display them on my bathroom wall as a reminder. Why? Because no one is perfect. God gave us laws to follow because often we do get out of line. You can appease every group out there, and I see certain corporations are giving millions to the cause. But, until you obey the laws of GOD, the money is going down the toilet. Yes, in the flusher. Petty men bring on selfish agendas because THEY believe it should be so. Take a refresher course in the TEN COMMANDMENTS. If the agenda doesn't line up, it's not in HIS plan. HAVE a thought-provoking Sunday and Shine!!!

August 30th

What an opportunistic time to Shine! Become a lighthouse in the storm. Lighthouses serve a purpose not only during times of storms but also during times of darkness. They alert sailors to hazards and guide their ships to safe harbors. Navigating the hazards of this virus has not been easy. How can one person lighten the burden? Be an example for those around you. YOU have outstanding opportunities to do good by transforming someone's frown into a smile! Tomorrow your assignment is to go out of your way and show kindness to everyone around you. Let your heart soar with the possibility that YOU are one of many wonderful changes in the world. Pass the baton, banish the darkness. One by one we can get it done! Shine, Shine, Shine!!!

Footnote: "Constant kindness can accomplish much. As the sun makes ice melt, kindness causes misunderstanding, mistrust, and hostility to evaporate." -Albert Schweitzer.

September 2nd a.m.

What is to come? In the distance I see the king, a bonny-bright moon holding court over night. As the sun rises, the queen - an eye-catching blazing sun - dismisses the king and takes over. Wallah - yesterday is a memory; today is a mystery unraveling. Mankind has always sought to unfold the future. On one hand, we'd like a peek into the future, but it might reveal facts we do not care to know, like the song, "Que sera, sera; whatever will be, will be." So take one day at a time. Somewhat comparable to the ending of a book or a movie. It's important to know how the story got there. The fear mongers continue to foresee the sky is going to fall. But my advice is to experience each moment as we discover the flow of our lives. Don't forget your dreams. The clock is ticking; get on with life! My heart is like a racehorse galloping on to a triumphant beat. A gamble for sure; but if you don't buy a ticket, how can you win? Bring on the day; let the race begin. Tally ho, Shine!!!

September 2nd p.m.

ARE YOU WHERE YOU NEED TO BE? This question happens to be paramount for me. Success is identifying where that place is. First, realize you may have to let go of baggage, then you are free to determine your destination. Bazinga! A mail truck drives by me and I feel a tweak of my past drive by. Visiting my oldest son (who lives right across the street from where he grew up), I realize this is not my neighborhood now. The past doesn't belong to me anymore. I am blessed where I am today. Home isn't a building; home is within our soul where peace, security and beauty live. I am no longer in search of the physical, rather the spiritual. I am in the BEST place I've ever been. I am flourishing and you can too! Know where you need to be and SHINE ON!!!

September 4th a.m.

It's 6:13 a.m. I've been to the GYM, back home and ready for a spin ON LIFE. Life is like playing musical chairs: You never know when the music will stop and someone else will be sitting in your chair. Yes, there is a virus; yes, there is an election. But I am reflecting on how precious our time on earth is. Practice kindness, be firm in your beliefs, and above all else, be authentic. Yeah, I believe we can achieve what we strive for without hurting anyone in our path, just keep it wide with love and pride. And don't forget to thank GOD that you are alive! Now approach the day with a positive attitude and zest, fulfilling your quest to Shine!!!

Footnote: Will a vaccine may be available before the election? Don't hold your breath. Reports say it may not be available until early 2021.

September 4th p.m.

Young people living today do not realize how blessed they are.
Given what they have, they seem to demand more. Do they realize many who came before them had less? Yet, they stilled thanked God for everything they had. At a young age during the depression, my father and uncle had to labor alongside my grandfather on their farm. One season, they had a surplus of a certain crop. My grandfather told them to pick out something from the Sears catalog, and when the check arrived, he would place the order. The family loaded up the harvest and transferred it to a train for delivery. Life moved at a slower pace then. My father and uncle were counting the days. One boy would run to the mailbox and it became the highlight of the day. The letter arrived, but a check was not inside. The letter explained the shipment got derailed and the food spoiled. Enclosed was a bill for the cleanup! Another time I remember my uncle telling me he wanted a toy car at the five and dime that cost a quarter. His parents told him they did not have the money. Despite the hard times, the boys grew up to be fine young men and served in WW2. They were patriotic, respected their country, and took good care of their parents till their deaths, only one year apart from each other. I am not saying all the youth today are ungrateful. God has blessed our culture. But many find fault with what is. When I think of Labor Day, I remember all those who came before me and how hard they toiled. They were so thankful to live and worship in the

greatest country on earth. And yes, I believe it is. I love this country! The festive and solemn holidays, honoring those who sacrificed much for our freedom. Friends, enjoy the Labor Day weekend and count your blessings! Decorate with red, white, and blue and SHINE!!!

September 5th

At the gym, we often talk about the CORE. Because working on our abs is fundamental. These deep muscles are where our strength comes from. Well now, permit me to talk about our inner core, that which exists inside our soul. Tough days in our country, with on-the-spot news of discord. It can be gut wrenching, struggling to sort out our inner thoughts. The media's targeting everyone: young, old, and people of all color. And often, because we identify with a group, our feelings nest there. Is it a good thing or a bad thing? Bad if we become victims, adopt hate and become the story. It's so important to remember what resonates in our core, because our core defines who we are. Yes, I see the perpetrators of evil who hide behind the veil of justice. Many of us know right from wrong - God help those who don't. Evil wants to peek in your soul and take up residence. Our core becomes weakened if we invite retaliation into our hearts. Peace to every one of you, left or right; let's treat each other with respect. Beef up your core and Shine!!!

September 10th

This week in men's bible study, we talked about how patient God is. Face it, friends, I don't know about you, but sometimes I would love to send a thunderbolt down on certain people! But we do not have privy to other people's inner thoughts, so judge not. The saying, "GOD is slow to anger" needs to be forefront in our minds. Allow someone to determine your emotions and you are smack dab out of the game. I want to get it right, don't you? Lord, give me patience and give it to me right now. Why? People are not following the rules. Society is pointing fingers at who to blame for the virus. My prayer is that I have PATIENCE to be the man I am under the mask, doing the task - not to preach, but able to teach, just being LIKE YOU trying to endure these days with genuineness. Wishing everyone a super productive day. "Thou shall love thy neighbor as thyself" is the second greatest commandment Jesus gave us. Banish thunder bolts from your mind. Shine on with patience and love for your neighbor!!!

Footnote: Problems cropped up in the third phase of a vaccine for the virus in the U.S. The vaccine has been put on hold at this time.

September 11th

As we age, we often reflect on things we did and things we did not do. One of my favorite pastimes is watching vintage movies, and one of my favorites is 1961's "Splendor in the Grass." This Hollywood film is based on the title of William Wordsworth's ageless poem. The movie is about two young people who fall in love and the complications that occur with dysfunctional families. When I was young, older people were always talking about how fast time flies. As a kid, I wondered how could that be? Especially when it took forever for Christmas to roll around again. Now, in a blink of an eye, it's a new year. How did I become "grandfather" material overnight? The words of the poem read, "Though nothing can bring back the hour." Yes, it's a closed chapter. A clock has three hands: one indicates seconds, the other indicates minutes and the third indicates hours. A bible quote in the King James version says, "Accept what is, let go of what was, have faith in what will be." In my current job, I thrive when working alongside young people. I am interested in their plans and am encouraging to a fault. Would I have changed anything in my life? Yes, without a doubt! But my choices brought me where I am today, a pleasant place interwoven with unexpected surprises and perks. In a special place, there is a box of pictures that span my lifetime. On rare occasions, I take them out and relive the past. I remember that young man and grin. Now in my mirror, a mature man smiles back at me. My focus is on today. The past is the past.

I will grieve not, rather find strength in what remains behind. And my message for today is: Revel in the moment and SHINE on to a splendorous day!!!

Footnote: It has been 19 years since a series of coordinated deadly terrorist attacks in the United States. On 12/18/2001, Congress approved to commemorate the anniversary by naming September 11th "Patriot Day," honoring American patriots who stepped up to the plate demonstrating tremendous courage during rescue efforts. May all the lives lost never be forgotten!!!

September 12th

Another classic movie that struck a chord in my heart is "Cat On a Hot Tin Roof." I can tell you I've been that cat on the hot tin roof of life many times. I am sure some individuals thought I'd fold. Have you ever felt that way? Without question, my faith helped me get me off that roof. GOD has always been my very dear friend. People complain about others having the life of Riley. Who said life would be a cakewalk? Some appear to get all the breaks. But I'll be the first to say, grab it and run with it while you can. For most, it's a negotiation process, taking what happens and making it work. And being thankful for what is. Aha, the attitude of gratitude goes a long way. When I hear "they owe me this" nonsense, I want to say, "life owes us nothing." Do not waste time complaining when you can accomplish something useful. Remember this is coming from a sixty-four-year-old man pushing shopping carts in the parking lot, many a time at high noon at a hundred degrees in the shade. And might I add, I am ever so thankful I can do it. In our neighborhood, homeowners are replacing their roofs with metal or tin. This brings a smile to my face and my advice to cats in the area: Caution kids stay off the roof and SHINE on to a grounded Saturday!!!

Footnote: "Cat on a Hot Tin Roof" was a 1958 drama starring Elizabeth Taylor, Paul Newman, and Burl Ives. A movie filled with symbolism's that explore family relationships, disappointments of aging and fears of death.

September 13th

Hey friends, a new week is on the horizon bringing some excellent opportunities to SHINE. Take the time to consider what you are lacking, fill in the blanks and promote the finest you. Encourage others to follow you. Spur one another on to do good deeds. Sometimes when you do good, it may boomerang back in your direction. Yes, expect, visualize, and receive. Don't wait for the other shoe to drop. Waltz into Monday as if you own it. "Waltzing Matilda, Waltzing Matilda, who'll come a Waltzing Matilda with me?" Sing till you SHINE!!!

Footnote: "Waltzing Matilda" was one of my mother's favorite Aussie songs. The phrase "Waltzing Matilda" means to travel from place to place with all one's belongings on their back. With the Aussie slang and phrases this is a catchy and lighthearted song, but in reality, it is the story of poverty and deprivation of nomadic laborers during the 1890's Depression.

September 15th

I haven't written lyrics to a song yet, but if I did it might start out, "Hang on to your Heart." By that I mean keep all the love, compassion, drive for life and the interest of people in your life going strong. Maybe in 2020, all the stress brought people to the end of their ropes when dealing with others. And if you throw in political preferences in the mix, it's like a powder keg waiting to explode. Don't allow situations and circumstances to dictate who you are. Some people like cats, other's dogs. So what? We can all still go to lunch together and I will even leave the tip. Live each day fulfilling your legacy. Find peace, love and happiness in your life and Shine on!!!

September 20th

In a matter of hours, this weekend will be history! I watched music videos from the 70's and 80's. It was a sweet and exciting time. Today I went to the grocery store and talked with a co-worker from my previous career. He informed me he has a few years before retirement. Wished him well as I reminisced about my years working there. At my age, it should be easy to retire and leave it all behind. Funny, I'm still trying to find my niche - somewhere to go, something to do. Have to keep on keeping on. Sad to hear about the death of a Supreme Court Justice. I admired her tenacity, working far into her golden years. Although our ideas may have been different, she was - in my mind - a hero. There is no expiration date on our drive, mission, and dreams. Tomorrow is on the horizon; carpe diem! Monday morning blues; no such mindset here. Shining on with tenacity!!!

Footnote: You have already embraced your present calling, to offer words of encouragement and hope - they are fuel to the soul and calmness to the mind. You are a rare gem that speaks powerful spirit driven words to help us get to the finish line. In this dark world, it is not a daily thing to read these words from mainstream media. Shine on, Steve, in your God-given purpose!

*****This comment was from one of my friends in my Shine Time group on Facebook. It meant so much to hear these words. I, like everyone else, have my ups and downs and sometimes doubt my present calling.*

September 21st

I'm looking at my glorious garden as the day surrenders to the night. So thankful for experiences I had on this wondrous day! In my life, I feel an urge to relish every moment like a child at Christmas. I want to tear into my present and move on to the next. My heightened awareness tells me to be careful with my words, thoughts and actions. Every day, we should sit and review our actions: what did we say, how did we say it? Remember, actions speak louder than words. Think about it. Perhaps many of us would benefit from making improvements? It's one of my new goals. Go on, turn the page and be on your best behavior. SHINE on to looking at your life through the eyes of a child!!!

Footnote: There are 'victories' and 'defeats' in everyday life. Wise are those who celebrate the victories and learn from the defeats. It's the outcome that measures the product. Pay attention to the recipe.

September 23rd

Well guys and girls, I know I'm always talking about TIME, but Thursday is on the horizon. Ready to wrap up another week as it goes into the history books in a blink of the eye. I can't tell you how anxious my soul has become. It's like a fast-moving train. I'm looking out the windows, trying to take it all in. The virus has stolen my life. Holidays and seasons have become hidden like the sun behind the clouds on a rainy day. Things have come to a dead stop, yet time is marching on. I've lost precious animals and a dear friend in 2020. I cannot deny the urge to move forward. Time, they say, waits for no man. I work tomorrow and am looking forward to seeing my world up front and personal. My wish for each and every one of you is to find your path and fill it with love and happiness! Go forth and tackle the day. It's your TIME to SHINE!!!

Footnote: Most of us are ordinary people living ordinary lives. I mean, come on, I'm bagging groceries. But when we decide to live our lives in an extra-ordinary way, extraordinary thing happen!

September 24th

Dear friends, as I've said before, we live in an age of instant news. The ramifications of these horrible stories playing out turn many of our hearts inside out. I find solace in what God reveals in the Bible: "Vengeance is mine." He will vindicate the righteous and punish the wicked. This has become planet Earth's biggest and most dangerous flaw: misguided human beings who feel they are in charge of judgment, not God. Sometimes in my life I have welcomed those thoughts for a moment, but those thoughts allow HATE to step in and take up residence in our hearts and soul. We can't afford the company, for hate will destroy everything, including ourselves if we allow it. Don't just flee...resist hate with every fiber in your body. Here and there around us, we perceive the fruits of hate. The fires of hell on earth propagate destruction. Believe me, these things are not from God, rather from the ancient evil one. Ever since creation, the devil has been at war with those created by GOD for His glory. Remember, we are only pilgrims passing through this planet. There IS a better, perfect place; only LOVE will get us there. Keep your lamps filled with oil because our salvation can be at dawn. Shine on with solidity and respect with an aim to eradicate the darkness of hate!!!

Footnote: There was a time when evil hid behind the wall to do the deeds. Now it's right out in front and easy to be seen, yet so many refuse to acknowledge its presence either because of political correctness or because it fits their agenda. These are difficult days indeed! Remember, if the state of affairs does not align with the word of GOD it is unacceptable.

September 26th

One of the greatest abilities one can possess is the ability to LISTEN and RESPECT someone whose opinions differ from yours. These days, from all sides, people ridicule and mock anyone who disagrees with them. I talk with many who whisper in fear rather than tell someone their point of view. ISN'T THIS AMERICA where FREE SPEECH is—was—supposed to dwell? These five words sum it up for me: I understand how you feel. Working with the public has given me an education in life. I'm glad there is diversity because it's what makes the world go round. Funny to say, I am a conservative and I'm a liberal; wouldn't have it any other way. Demonstrate common sense sprinkled with respect and you'll be FINE porcupine! Shine on!!!

September 27th

Fear can take many of us to different places; it has been a constant unwelcome companion of mine for most of my life. Allow fear inside your heart and soul and you will lose the anchor of your security. The virus has painted 2020 with fear. Many people feel lost. Today at a store, a young woman was buying Halloween materials, and I told her it made me happy that holidays were being planned. Inch by inch, I hope and pray confidence will return, confidence to live our lives without fear. Soon we will take our masks off and see those beautiful smiles. Oh yes, friends, we've all been to different places, even stuck in our homes. We've been living with fear too long. Onward and upward, a new week awaits! Bright and beautiful colors to view and experience as we soon travel into October. Shine on because The Great Pumpkin is on the way!!!

September 28th

Wouldn't it be marvelous if we could listen, affirm, serve, and be kind to each other? Black, white, gay, straight, this faith, that faith - let's strive to live in peace. I'll be the FIRST to admit I don't have all the answers, but I'll tell you this: I'm blessed to work in the public eye where I can reach out to everyone I come in contact with. And when I say hello and have a great day, I MEAN EVERY WORD! I'm not banging my drum, but all I can say is give peace a chance. Hats off to all the average Joe's. I may not be on the cover of a magazine or on the news, but this little cricket is chirping a song of Zip-A-Dee-Doodah. Come on, join me! Kindness is the key that unlocks the door. You want things to be better? Start with yourself. Bring it on and spread it around. It may surprise you how a tiny spark of energy can SHINE up the world; dare ya!!!

September 29th

Well friends, tonight is the great presidential debate. Who will emerge the proposed winner? I wouldn't tell anyone who to vote for; I prefer to comment on a perspective for the winners and losers. It's marvelous to be a winner, devastating to be a loser. Been there and back, and it blows - like being picked last for a team! Humiliation is the worst thing to experience. Not the end of the story, though. Many pick themselves up by the bootstraps and travel back into the swamp with determination. Never look at anyone and think loser. GOD created each one of us with distinct talents. The formula is finding out our strengths and claiming them. Hidden victories come out of people no one expected had it in them. Never close the book on anyone, including yourself. Expect a brand-new chapter. I've told you I dislike discussing politics. I do have my choice, but I wish BOTH of them well. Find your true calling and blessings will be bestowed. Popcorn, please; I'll be watching. SHINE ON TO A SUPER TUESDAY!!!

September 30th

Do any of you mature people remember this 1966 hit song, "They're Coming to Take Me Away, Ha-Ha?" The world might be at this point. Maybe it's in the air or water. Who knows! Seems like everyone's losing it, except for me - or so I say. These days I spend my time talking to animals. See a guy in the front yard conversing with a wild rabbit? That's me. "How are you doing today?" I ask. Is Covid driving us all to the brink? We need a return to the simple days of yesterday. I'd love to have a retro den with an old TV and play all those old funny sitcoms. Such innocent times. I remember the thrill of watching The Wonderful World Of Disney about this time of the year. Many choices to view on TV today, but it's come with a hefty price tag. They would not like me to show up at the funny farm. I'd have everyone dancing and having a good time! Possibilities are everywhere if you look for them. I gave the rabbit a name...Harvey. Can't wait to talk with him later! Hats off to a hilarious Wednesday: ha-ha, ho-ho, he-he - Shining is elemental!!!

October 1st

Be brave, my friends! Gallant enough to design your own dreams and believe in them before they slip away. Remember this: tomorrow is only a day away. Keep your flag flying high and your sight on the prize, for when the morning light comes, new possibilities arrive! Shine on with infinite HOPE for the future!!!

Footnote: The president and first lady have tested positive for the Coronavirus. On Friday, the president was taken to the Walter Reed National Military Medical Center for treatment due to Covid complications. The first lady remains in the White House without serious complications.

October 3rd

Today on a lighter note: Saturday nights bring back fond memories of my unadulterated youth. My parents loved The Lawrence Welk Show. My sister and I dominated the TV except for Saturday nights when this show came on. I hated it; so did my sibling. Today I have a contrary opinion. But I'd love a second chance to be with my parents. Life has changed from those uncomplicated days. Our family had one TV and a small living room, a black and white world back then. I remember when our neighbor bought the first color TV on the block. We rushed over to see the show, "My Mother, the Car." The tints were kinda green, but we "oohed" and "ahhhed." Today people have both family and media rooms and several televisions. I feel that this exposes children to a barrage of information. Aren't they growing up way too fast? You should relish childhood and the time you spend with your parents. I think of my parents often. Looking forward to a laid-back Sunday. Friendship, love and happiness to all of you. "A-one and a-two..." You SHINE, Lawrence Welk!!!

Footnote: The first episode of the Lawrence Welk Show aired on May 11, 1951 (before I was born) and ended on April 17, 1982. It was a musical variety show. The host was a musician, accordionist and bandleader. Remembered for Bubbles in the Wine and his Champagne Music, Welk was posthumously inducted into the International Polka Music Hall of Fame in 1994.

October 4th

Where does happiness come from? I wish I knew. Wouldn't you want to be first in line if someone was handing it out? There is a term relating to money, referred to as lean times. Perhaps the term might relate to happiness in our lives. We've all had glorious moments of pure bliss before lean times sneak back in like a thief in the night. It's not always about us. Happiness intertwines with loved ones in the fabric of our lives. Unhappiness can come out of left field and hit you hard. I wish I had a magic wand so I could send happiness out to everyone on planet Earth. I believe happiness grows in the heart with gratitude. UN-happiness starts with not having everything we desire. Even at my age, many of my dreams haven't even scratched the surface. But I'm over the moon for everything I have. Alas, with the reality that perhaps what I desire is not for meant me. Where does happiness vibrate? Does it begin the mind, sink into the gut and filter over to the heart? At 64, I'm working on my body so if the mind ever gets there, the body might help make it happen. Never, ever give up on possibilities for your future! Keep dreaming. For as you dream, you shall become. I wish you happiness - tons and tons of it. Shovel it into a wheelbarrow and SHINE!!!

Footnote: On October.6th the president was released from the hospital and returned to his residence in the White House. Is he out of the woods yet? Time will tell. Next on the agenda is the vice-presidential debate tomorrow night.

October 8th

Random thoughts from a random day. One of my friend's appearance is perfect and he seems to have his life in perfect order. Is my life in perfect order? No, I am neither perfect nor organized. My crazy mind tells me there is hope. I keep my underwear and sock drawer in impeccable order. I can be proud of that...right? But perfect is as perfect does. A little insanity comes in handy. Strive for excellence this Friday because even if you fall short you will continue to Shine!!!

October 10th a.m.

You know, everyone wants to feel they are right about their values, beliefs and their faith. Perhaps it is part of our human nature because it seems right to be right. But at what price? Insisting that you are right, and someone is wrong, can get way out of control. And I, for one, don't like it. I can remember riding on the school bus when I was a young boy and arguing with another kid over the make of a car. Childish, but I was just a child. What are the excuses today for some grown adults behaving as children? And, I might add, spoiled children. Look, debates are just that, but afterwards let's agree to disagree in a friendly manner. You may like praline ice cream; I like mint chocolate chip. Doesn't society put a lid on diversification by diffusing the differences? Are they trying make everyone into the same product? It does not work. Diversity makes the world go round. BELIEVE in what motivates you to be a better person. But please don't shove it down anyone's throat. These days I'm wearing a mask for several hours and I'm clogged up enough! Celebrate what's unique about you and what's unique about your neighbor. Place your best foot forward on Saturday and you will SHINE!!!

October 10th p.m.

My late, dear father said toward the end of his life that he had no regrets and would live his life all over and never change a thing. Bless him, but I might change a thing or two. One glaring fact is that I am driven. Now, if you were to access my accomplishments, you might not agree. Never finished college, no degree, no trophies or awards of any kind. Still, I've lived a busy life and worked very hard. Maybe like you have? Ordinary here but striving to never waste a minute. I'm not a mathematician, but my body can calculate the years. Driven to deliver the best product called me, but sometimes I feel I work way too hard at it. I should space things out. And try to understand checks and balances. That's my latest project, easing back a bit and finding the essence of what is important. Sliding into home base rather than running full speed ahead. Gotta chill, my friends, going to chill. Sunday - going to make it a fun day; hope you will too, friends. SHINE ON, SHINERS!!!

October 12th

This has been one HECK of a tough year for everyone. The coronavirus has put the brakes on moving ahead from children to adults. I thought it would be a piece of cake to stay home and sequester. I discovered that it's not the ideal situation if you are a social person. So many lives and dreams became quarantined. Most of the states have moved from stay-at-home orders to easing restrictions. Fears of secondary outbreaks are materializing. Still, we cannot let this virus hold us hostage. Crude but true: get off the pot and get moving. Hit the gas pedal and merge back into traffic. FOCUS on what you can accomplish. If you need to wear a mask, do it. Dust off the cobwebs and get cracking! Even if your desire is waning, do it anyhow. Rely on your FAITH and lasso the moon like George Bailey did in the movie, "It's A Wonderful Life." Jimmy Stewart's character, while in the worst of times, found the best of times. The clock is ticking. Covid may have slowed things down, but time has other ideas. I am ever so grateful that my first book, Conversations From The Porch, was published in June of 2020. It was filled with nostalgia. I felt compelled to write my second book due to the panic and fear the virus unleashed. My attitude is all about shining and promoting positivity. My goal is to snuff out the negative. FOCUS on what motivates you! Come on, find your energy and share it with our world. Within you lies the gift. Use it, share it, and SHINE!!!

Footnote: "It's a Wonderful Life" is one of my favorite classic Christmas movies! This movie was released in 1947 and based on the short story and booklet, The Greatest Gift, which Philip Van Doren Stern published in 1943.

October 14th

MEMORIES...they can be heavenly, or they can be HELL. Sometimes my mind beats me up because of all the MISTAKES I made along the journey. Sad to realize I have disappointed people along the way, but with God's forgiveness, every one of us can start all over again. So take out your eraser and dust off the chalk. Sometimes we can't always make it up to the people we've let down. If we can, it's wonderful. Age has taught me the real things in life that are important. Sharing what we can to all we encounter. There are seven gifts of the Holy Spirit: Wisdom, understanding, counsel, fortitude, knowledge, piety, and fear of the Lord. Dear God, help us learn the value of why we are here and live it. Friends, let your LOVE Shine on to brighten someone's day!!!

October 16th

MESSAGE OF THE DAY: We are all placed on earth to help and assist our fellow man on the journey ahead. So do the right thing. Treat each other with respect and dignity. LIFE cannot just be about you; it's a shared duty. Strive for an experience of a LIFETIME. Walk in love and SHINE with abundance!!!

Footnote: HAPPINESS IS LIKE REAL ESTATE. IT'S ALL ABOUT LOCATION. Search properties with ample room for love. Then seek out a simple curiosity for life itself. Locate what motivates your soul!!!

October 18th

Today's thought: Father Time. Aging is like a roller coaster ride. It takes quite a while to make it to the top of the ride, but time flies on the way down. As we approach the golden years, it is just an illusion that time speeds up. Not a bad thing. On a faster track, don't we hurry to grasp opportunities before they slip through our fingers? My heart soars with gratitude for every day I am blessed to receive. So refrain from complaining. Accept what is and work with it. Don't look back at yesterday. I'm on a mission to re-invent myself to fit into the current picture. On an antique dresser are photos of days gone by, I remember that guy, but I like this guy better. Make every day count. Age gracefully and you will Shine!!!

October 20th

One significant word that sums up SUCCESS for growing older: ADAPTABILITY. Doesn't this apply to life too? In life, it's difficult to accept change. Or to adopt what change brings. STEER changes in the right direction. Then the pieces come together. Let me give you a comparison. A jacket covered with dust lurked in my closet. I loved this jacket; it used to fit me like a glove. Years passed and the jacket no longer fit. One day, I released my attachment to it. Once was no longer here; time had the upper hand. Successful people distinguish between past and present. Time can teach you wonderful lessons. The cooler weather is approaching. I'm looking for a new jacket. Seasons are open to change; are you? Try to go with the flow. Grow and your adaptability will SHINE!!!

Footnote: Reminder… BY ALL MEANS WEAR A MASK OVER YOUR MOUTH BUT NOT OVER YOUR HEART! Let our love for each other be stronger than any virus. Sprinkle love here there and everywhere you go.

October 22nd

A post I saw disturbed me big time. A popular performer had her picture taken in front of an image representing a presidential candidate and displayed a rude gesture. OK, we know her opinion, and it's great to express our opinions. But crude, vulgar gestures are not acceptable. Has our society sunk to being depraved? Are we teaching our young it's fine to behave like this? Yeah, I'm on a soapbox. If our nation falls prey to this mindset, we will lose reverence in the shuffle! Isn't common decency a foundation for a healthy society? Otherwise, we are heading for destruction big time. My late father laid it on the line: "If you have nothing nice to say, say nothing at all." I don't give a hoot about anyone's celebrity status. This behavior is plain "gutter-talk." Money, fame, and position means nothing if grace, dignity and respect do not accompany it forward. Words and actions relay who we are. Please, everyone, use them wisely. Be a SHINING example for the youth in our country!!!

October 22nd

Occasionally we get a small, tiny chance to play God. For days, a small lizard became trapped in my bathroom. Several times I've tried to capture him. Have there been times in your life when you went to places you shouldn't have gone? How many times has our loving God rescued you? Many times for me. I prayed I could rescue this creature from harm. Today I did. I hope he thrives in the sun where he will SHINE!!!

October 23rd

In my hometown there lived a famous flashy woman. A local celebrity of sorts who hobnobbed with the wealthy jet-set. Someone asked her if she believed in FATE. "YES, but you need to show up." It kinda makes sense to me. I see patterns where life sent me into directions I did not expect. Do what you feel you're called to do, then leave it to the higher source. Somehow, and often mystical, we are all participants in our fate. How much can we claim was because of our choices? Someone else holds the blueprints. Have a great Saturday and show up. You never know where the stardust may fall. SHINE!!!

October 29ᵗʰ

SUPERNATURAL THOUGHTS: Since this is a Halloween week, I am hitting on some 'scary thoughts.' My parents raised me in a wonderful religion with strict beliefs. But I am also a person who exists outside the box. Take, for instance, the spirit world. The flesh and spirit worlds run parallel, and a fine line appears to separate them. One movie that struck a serious cord with me was "Ghost." I believe there is a spirit world operating on earth. I once lived in a house where strange things happened, but I never felt afraid. The Bible says that we fight not with the flesh, rather with powers and principalities. I agree. The spirit world is at war. Though I've never seen an angel, I believe angels are among us. In the body-building world, you take vitamins and supplements to keep your flesh strong and at maximum performance. Spiritually, we need to keep the word of the living GOD in our hearts and souls to be strong. Because I am a sensitive soul, I perceive repercussions in the undercurrents. It's a heavy price to pay, and yes, I often have to come to terms with it; it's why I work so hard to keep the love going. The lines between flesh and spirit are intersecting more than ever. Energies vibrate like a volcano preparing to erupt. The rumblings are clear to those sensitive souls. Planet Earth is going into an unprecedented war. Therefore, it's very important to guard your heart, soul and mind more than ever before. Being in the flesh encapsulated by the spirit within; perhaps the secret is balance. When you encounter hate, let the alarm go off. Don't cross the line. Shine on in universal peace and love.

October 31st

My goal is to post upbeat thoughts. Today, please permit me to bring in a somber reflection. We are, as a nation, most times dependent upon our government to supply our needs. Colossal mistake. The day after this election, whatever the outcome, will not bring immediate peace, prosperity and happiness. All the flaws will still be there. Man alone cannot handle the problems of a fallen world; only GOD can. Peace begins from within. Act, believe, and live it. We cannot rely on prosperity in monetary results. One of the happiest persons I ever came across was my father. He cared little about money. He found joy in the simple things. Abundant happiness comes from the soul. Only YOU can define where you find it. Yes, elections are important. Do not put your faith in man. Seek it from within and let it SHINE. LIFE will go on; bring your happiness along!!!

November 1st

Today's Thought: Wow, what a discombobulated political season this has been for our country! It brought out the ugly in many. Here is my take. I think by now you suspect my choice. I own it, no apologies. But don't knock anyone else down to get your point understood. I've never experienced a season like this, and I hope I never experience it again. Violence against opposite ideas, beliefs, and having the cowardice view that one can still be a liberal thinker and misbehave. No, you can't. What's wrong will always be wrong. There are no excuses on God's earth to act like this. Rioting, looting and acts of violence are ALL WRONG and EVIL. I've heard well-educated folk saying they understand; I don't. My parents raised me to know better. To tear down statues, desecrate churches, and paint streets with symbols of power - how disgraceful! Still, it is important to listen and try to repair the past. I cannot say I understand how some people feel; I have never walked in their shoes. What makes a country great? The happiness of its citizens. Family makes room for everyone at the table. I am not psychic; who knows what Tuesday will bring? Whatever happens, bring a larger table into the room. Use both ears to listen. Our country has seen many seasons before; we can take on this one too. Yes, stand up for your beliefs, but do it with respect, compassion, and with honor toward your fellow citizen. GOD BLESS AMERICA. May our flag SHINE from sea to shining sea!!!

November 2nd

Flaws: Reality 101. At my gym, there are mirrors everywhere and everywhere. Some may love them, some may hate them, and some live with them. A person asked the late actress Mae West why she had a mirror over her bed. "I Wanna see how I'm doing!" she exclaimed. Um, yes, but here's my take on them. Mirrors keep me ever so humble. We all have pluses and minuses. Add and subtract and there you go; the total is YOU! Embrace them, don't erase em; it's the human you. Do you like the person called YOU - FLAWS and all? I'm here and it's a pretty good place to be. It's the LOVE in the heart and the JOY of living that defines happiness. Don't allow the mirror the last word. Like what you look at and live your truth. Shining all the way to the gym!!!

Footnote: Every day is a challenge. Be a "BETTER" person than you were yesterday. Out do 'yourself' and SHINE!!!

November 4th a.m.

Trump or Biden, where ya siden? Not to worry; don't flee or scurry, cry or moan. Remember, GOD IS ON HIS THRONE. What is will be; life goes on. Keep doing the right thing. Be a good citizen in your world. Because within our own small part of the universe, our true purpose lies. SHINE ON SHINER'S! I know you can do it!!!

November 4th p.m.

My OWN OPINION piece: I own it, not sour grapes. Just the way I see things, not up for debate. Well, it looks to me like the left has won the election in 2020. They've almost got their guy across the finish line. Never in my life have I seen the general media present itself as biased. Negative stories about their guy kept from the spotlight. And 'hurling' everything but the kitchen sink at our president. I do not dislike former Vice President, Mr. Biden. If I had the chance to sit and talk with Biden, I think we'd get along. But I am preparing myself for the future. Expecting a strong docket to show its face soon. A movement of change that some will like, and others will not. We are the greatest country ever to exist, hands down. You won't find me out on the streets protesting. I will not loot or steal or vandalize. I am an old man set in his ways. Steadfast in what is right and wrong. And a firm believer in one true GOD. I grew up in a democratic family. Pictures of the late John F. Kennedy were on the walls of my boyhood home. I do not recognize that party now. In my naivety, I hope we can all work together in peace and in harmony. On the flip side, good luck with that one. Will I respect our new president? Yes, absolutely. I intend to be a good citizen. But I'll be carrying an umbrella of truth over my head. Why? Because I see storm clouds in the distance. Remember the saying, "Be careful what you wish for, you might just get it?" A government cannot give you peace. As I've said before, PEACE starts with you and me.

I hope we will settle differences and work together, right or left. Let peace begin with us so the American flag can SHINE on!!!

Footnote: "Change is the law of life. And those who look only to the past or the present are certain to miss the future"- John F. Kennedy.

November 6th

Rooted in my front garden is an Orchid tree. Most of the year it looks quite bland. Nothing to write home about. But during this time of the year, it blooms. Many neighbors along the way often stop. One kind lady told me it was her favorite tree in the entire neighborhood. How so are many of us? Blended into this world, most people see nothing special about us. But allow our genuine colors to shine from within and our hearts bloom, and all that is special about us takes note. Friends, I believe we ALL have unique, wonderful elements that GOD endowed us with. Share it with the world. Blooming colors light up our world and help us SHINE!!!

November 7th

The sun will come up tomorrow; life will go on. I'm not sure what we make happen and what fate makes happen. Perhaps it's a mix? Most people think they are in control. But are they? Part of the work is how we deal with it. God has given me lessons from day one and throughout my life. A neighbor who had two children discovered her husband walked out on her and she had to relinquish her beautiful home. At first, she and the children lived out of the family's station wagon. One day I saw her car drive by her former home. A new family occupied it. She stopped to talk with me. I mean, what a hero. Found a new job, rented an apartment, and survived the storm. It struck a chord in my heart. Many years later, I still admire her. She did what she had to do. I never saw her again, but still her story is written in my files. Accepting defeat does not always equate to failure, it just means you may have to make adjustments, rearrange things, and let go. Friends, find the strength that has been inside you all along. Look for the sun to come up. Life will go on; so shall we. SHINE in the face of hard knocks!!!

November 9th

I have a wonderful neighbor, and throughout this election we were on opposite sides. And maintaining ultimate respect for each other. Well, today he brought over a pie for my family, one that he baked himself. Beyond anything, it shows me we are a diverse people, living together with respect despite our difference. By all means, stand firm in your beliefs, but allow room for other thought processes. We must go forth. It's up to you and up to me as to how we accomplish this. Maybe I'm a fluff, but I am a fluff that sticks to my beliefs. Doesn't everyone want to live in a productive world...a world with room for everyone...a world bringing respect and honor to the table? Mine has a delicious pie on it! Shine on and be a good neighbor!!!

November 10th

Ho, ho, ho, it's time for Christmas movies. My favorite network has the most predictable movies. I could write some; wish they would ask me! Anyhow, the plot involves a good-looking guy or girl from the city who has a wonderful high- paying job. He/she returns to the country and runs into another good-looking person (sometimes from the past). At first, it's a no-go, but then everything turns to gold at the end of the rainbow. Ridiculous, of course, but it makes us all happy. And why the heck not? Who needs actual life all the time? Sitcoms in the 60s revealed social issues, but the ending usually worked out. Then the 70s, 80s, 90s and the present rolled in. Movies took a left turn into ugly. I have to say, avoid the ugly...not because they aren't real, but I find the energies can drain you. I like a happy medium. There was a show back in the mid-late 70s that I loved called "Family." It was a fictional TV drama with realistic issues centering around sparks of love and hope, and - of course - trying to tell the story of what a real family means. When I was in California, I had my picture taken in front of the actual house that represented the show. Sometimes I look at it and smile. Back to my list of Christmas shows I will be a watching: Rudolph, Miracle on 34th St., and Christmas in Connecticut. Also going to tune in to good old Christmas tunes. Yeah, you might say I am a Christmas guy; but don't we all need a rest from reality? Wishing everyone the hap-happiest season of all! Shine on as bright as Rudolph's nose!!!

November 11th

Why did this happen to me? Good question. I will be the first to say you may never know why. Perhaps it's God's way of trusting that you will come to terms with it and show compassion for someone else who is going through a similar situation. Most neighbors might call me the happiest person on the block. This can drive some people nuts; sorry I am just built that way. However, I remember a dry patch in my life when depression descended upon me; didn't see it coming. I was stuck in a dark cloud surrounded by a dense fog. I never realized what some poor souls go through. My depression didn't last long, but it made me realize how disheartening it can be. Sometimes it might be a blessing to experience this situation. Maybe then we'd be slow to judge. I attended school with a guy who seemed to have everything: popular, handsome, and from a desired area to live in. Later he took his own life. Tragic ending. I try to treat everyone in my path with a patch of kindness and human reflection. We are all flawed creatures. So go easy on yourself and everyone else. Life is precious. God has everyone here for a reason. Let today's prayer be: God, help me show respect to everyone I encounter. We may not understand their journey, but we should strive to be a light for them on the passage through life. SHINE!!!

November 12th

The holidays are here, and I get reminiscent of days gone by, remembering my loved ones who are no longer with me. And I miss innocent days of great anticipation. I'd love to have a den with a pleasant fragrant cypress and a fireplace and a retro TV that played all the old shows. I love all the Christmas shows from the past and sitcoms of the 60s. Maybe an antique jukebox stocked with 45's from the golden days. Wouldn't it be grand if our departed love ones could be here with us? I know, it's my crazy mind at play...but wouldn't it be awesome? Sounds like I'm looking for that genie in a bottle. Winter dreaming perhaps, so dream on, friends. It's beginning to look a lot like Christmas. And don't forget Thanksgiving. SHINE into the holidays!!!

November 13th

Life teaches me lessons every day. Like how little I know about anything. Our greatest flaw comes when we think our way is the only way. Rewards come when we stop to listen. Life invites us to a Smorgasbord. One needs to be open for everything on the table. I look for the deserts first; others like to WHINE and DINE. But my favorite thing to do is SHINE!!!

November 15th

Yesterday, a nice young woman came through my line at work.

She had a beautiful baby girl in her cart. I waved; the child gave me an uncertain expression. I said to the mother, "Does this mask must scare her?" The mother replied, "No, that's all she's known." My heart ached. Covid through a child's eyes. Nothing compares to giving and receiving smiles. Yes, a simple smile can transform our mood. It is imperative to wear a mask, one of many right things. Some are like taking a spoonful of bitter medicine. Don't buck the system; we are on overload. I'm less into news and striving to make myself a better person, be a responsible citizen and an active participant on GOD'S earth. Life is all about learning lessons. If 2020 wasn't a learning place, nothing will be. Let's all shift gears and slow down as we approach 2021. One valuable message for me… don't expect other people to paint your world; paint it yourself and decide what you want it to look like. The lessons SHINE on with all the colors of the rainbow!!!

Footnote: The Corona virus crisis in the U.S. continues with one million new cases, partial shutdowns, new restrictions and panic-buying. Wear a mask, use common sense, and don't ignore the possibility that you or your loved ones are at risk! Sacrifices need to be made during the holiday season to slow the spread. Hang on just a little bit longer because a vaccine is on the way.

November 16th

A STEP IN THE RIGHT DIRECTION. I can't recall which child it was, but one of my guys started crawling backwards. I thought it was funny. One needs to go forward to make documented progress. How often have you found yourself in that very position: Feeling stuck and not able to move forward no matter how hard you try? You don't like the results, but it's much easier to remain safe in your comfort zone. Won't work, nada, forget about it. Each day, our world spins forward. Days become nights, weeks become months, and years become decades. This year has been a tragedy, filled with great suffering, destruction, and death. The good news is that we will soon leave it in the past where it belongs. Stepping forward and leaving the past behind will not be easy for many, especially those who have lost loved ones. As painful as it has been, choosing movement over stagnation is essential. Life moves on. Yes, it may take enormous strength, but holding on to the past will create even more problems. Today I'm going to do some laundry and clean up my act. Doing simple things help get the cog in the wheel turning. Rainy days will always be in the forecast; it is part of life. So get under your umbrella and SHINE!!!

November 19th

What makes you happy? The most important question in your life and you OWN IT! I remember when I was a child at our church, an older lady who would spend hours cleaning out the votive candles. I thought she was nuts. "What a waste of time" was my childish reasoning. Now that I am older and wiser, I realize she seemed happy to do it. With age, we may have to compromise with what makes us happy. My late uncle loved to play golf. In his later years, he could no longer swing a club, but it thrilled him to watch golf on the television. What I'm trying to write here is finding what makes you happy is critical in your life. So work at finding that spot. Happiness is stronger than any drug; it's a supernatural force that improves our health by stimulating the brain. Yesterday I went out in my yard and saw many of my neighbor's yard crews mowing and weed whacking. They prefer having someone else do their yard work. But sculpting my bushes and shaping my plants into my own vision gives me purpose. Find what makes you joyful and everything else around you will bloom! Shine with a purpose in life!!!

November 21st

Today's Phrase: Despite everything, GIVE THANKS. Yes, chaos and fear surround the circumstances of 2020. I HONESTLY can't tell anyone FEAR NOT 'cause I have my moments. Blame the old "what if" conundrum? There's enough material to sew a gigantic circus tent out of the calamity. But, within my heart, I profess an overwhelming gratitude of thanks to GOD. At work, a man asked me, "What makes you happy?" My answer was TO BE ALIVE. So as we wind up our week towards THANKSGIVING, let's do some major rehearsals. If you like to sing…SING. If you prefer dancing…DANCE. And even if you feel silly, go for it. Believe me, it has never stopped me. Don't look in the menacing and sinister shadows. Follow the light and rejoice! Despite everything, God will provide for those that love Him. Love Him first; everything else will spring forth and you will SHINE!!!

November 25th

In my recent travels, I met a couple who were back-packing across America. Their companions included three animals they met along the way. The young man and woman were robust, energetic, and filled with hope. They had few belongings yet seemed happy and filled with enthusiasm. I always love talking with interesting people - such young hearts. A pang of loss hit me in the gut as I remembered long ago when my childish heart felt adventurous. Many people live in fear of being in close proximity with other people due to the virus. It is certainly understandable and necessary. The days of coming up close and talking with strangers have become taboo. It's a shame. I think my curiosity for what makes people tick will keep me young. Cannot wait until I can throw away my dreadful mask and smile. I hear the words in my head insist, "This too shall pass!" Amen to that. Tomorrow is Thanksgiving. We have much to be thankful for! SHINING on to turkey day…gobble, gobble!!!

Wearing a mask in this pandemic: I've let my beard grow out and it has become snow white. Something is telling me I'm entering the WINTER of my life and I revel with a grateful heart. Thankful for every moment! Dear friends, your life can't be a Hallmark moment every day, but every moment creates the place we exist today. For me, it's a pretty good place to be. Every person has taught me lessons. Have a blessed Thanksgiving day. Rejoice because your name is written in the Book of Life! Experience moments as rare and wonderful gifts. Like ornate crystal objects, they shine upon our lives with great beauty. Friends, realize one of the greatest gifts God has given us is the gift to LOVE. Cherish these moments and let them SHINE in your hearts!!!

November 27th

Accept responsibility for YOURSELF. We are living in a time where BLAME is circulating everywhere. "They did this, and they did that." Wake up, America - it ALL starts with us. I strive to do a daily review of my actions. In my heart, I know where I missed the mark. Humans are subject to flaws but realizing one can strive to do better helps soften the blow. That's life in a nutshell, so break it open; make some improvements. I take responsibility for my actions. Observing close up makes my review more personable. The recent political season has been a big drain and strain, then throw a virus into the mix and you have a recipe for disaster! Man, that's a whole 'lotta load' to carry around. It's early in the morning and still dark. I've already been to the gym. Hey, today I'm going to put forth my best shot. That's ALL anyone can do. Don't forget the desire needs to be the recipe. Be there. December is around the corner. SHINE on as we get one step closer to a vaccine!!!

November 28th

Thought for the day: Some say we are results of our upbringing.

I would agree to a certain degree, but after having children, I might say everyone is born with distinct personalities. My wife and I raised our children the same, but each of my sons are wired differently. God blessed me with wonderful parents. My siblings and I are also wired differently. We are our own creatures. Remembering my family life as a child, I cannot recall my parents having such a drive as I do. Maybe things were more laid back in their day. Do you ever drive yourself crazy with the things you do? This morning I opened the blinds to the dining room window to find it needs washing on the outside. Could I just relax and watch a morning show? No. I'll bring a bucket out in a few minutes. And ask my neighbors how many times I mow my lawn each week. It is how I am made! I love to mow, weed, and shape the plants. None of my children give a hoot about landscaping! But here I am, being me; and there you are, being you. Somewhere, some place, lies the blueprints. You are unique, one of a kind. Be yourself and SHINE!!!

November 29th

God's plans are awesome. He created us to be companions and helpers for each other. I'm one of those 'people' persons. I enjoy being around people. Now, with this pandemic manipulating the show, everyone needs to stay at a safe distance. This doesn't feel right to me; it goes against creation. But now it's necessary for creation to survive. This time will pass soon, especially since the first doses of the vaccine are expected to be approved before the end of 2020. Will anything good come from this catastrophe? Soon, the green light will come on. Perhaps we will value our fellow humans being more. To resume everyday activities seems like a long-lost dream. Hugs and talking side by side. Oh, how the beautiful smiles will emerge once the vaccine becomes a reality! Hang in there, friends. And when it happens, be ready TO SHINE!!!

November 30th

It's NEVER wrong to LOVE someone. Today I saw a picture of two young people in LOVE. It flooded my mind with precious memories. Adolescent love...ah, a forever, wonderful thing! I remember when my wife and I were first married. Yes, money was scarce, but with great anticipation we visited model homes. An older couple who bought a home in the complex invited us in to see theirs. The husband told us how very sentimental his wife was when she saw us - perhaps reminiscing about their early marriage years. Now, dear friends, it's my time to express my thoughts on love. I will say with confidence that it is never a mistake to love anyone, nor can anyone else sit in judgment. LOVE is a personal thing, owned in the heart by the one who loves. Falling in love is a most precious gift. The heart flutters, and magic happens when two hearts become as one. Never fear falling in love; fear not being able to SHINE!!!

December 1st

Yeah! December has arrived and we are sledding into Christmas.

Many years ago when I was a child, we had a drugstore near my house. A small diner was inside the store. In my mind, I still remember the taste of their awesome French fries. Back to my story. It was Christmas Eve. My mother needed to do some last-minute shopping, and I had to tag along. She told me to sit in a chair at the diner while she shopped. A waitress sitting next to me was counting out her change, most likely tip money for the day. I knew her because her son attended school with me. The single mother got up and proceeded down the cheap toy aisle (much like our dollar stores today). Looking at her change, she sorted out what toys (mostly plastic) she could get her children for Christmas. As a young boy, I don't think it affected me, but now, having been a parent, it breaks my heart. 2020 has been a tough year! I'll bet there are many parents counting their change. Let's make this a giving year. Give a little more on the tip list, make contributions to charities. This server may not have been a super star to other people, but to me, she was! Christmastime is the season of joy and one to share from our hearts! When we SHINE on others, our light becomes brighter than a Christmas tree!!!

December 2nd

Tonight our first "cold snap" arrived with blustery weather. I went to the closet to get my favorite blanket, a blanket my little love, my dog Muffin, loved so much. I touched the fabric and memories of her flooded my mind. Here is a poem dedicated in her memory.

> She was so much more than a dog to me; she was everything and more.
>
> This season came without you. A cold wind blew through and I thought about you.
>
> It's telling me there is a new season, but I'm sad   and you're the reason.
>
> I recall all the seasons we spent time together, in good and stormy weather. The two of us, inseparable.
>
> When I felt sick, you'd sleep by my side with one eye open. It was comforting to be there and pet you.
>
> I knew that somehow you knew what I was thinking. We had wonderful times. I remember looking at you, grinning and winking.
>
> You are always and forever in my heart. The days come and go, and so too come the seasons, filled with duty and untold beauty.
>
> Life must go on, it's true. I'm sad, I'm blue because this season has come without you!
>
> Till we meet on the Rainbow Bridge, Shine on!!!

Footnote: U.S. reports the largest number of deaths from the coronavirus since June. The UK issued emergency approval for coronavirus vaccine and expect distributions next week. Hopefully, here in the U.S., the first shipments of the vaccines are scheduled to be delivered in mid-December.

December 3rd

What's one amazing thing about writing? You can create the story the way YOU want it to go. Not at all like in actual life. Have I loved the way my personal story has played out? No, not always. Given the chance, I would change some chapters big time. But we get what we get. Yes, some things are our own choice; others come into play with the cards that life has given us. I feel I agreed to all this before. I know some would disagree. That's fine, okeydokey (spelled right or wrong, you get the point). Now comes the pitch: Whatever the story, it's how you decide to edit it and what you decide to get out of it that counts. Sometimes a chapter of your book runs dry. Don't throw the pages in the garbage can. The next chapter might be an answer to your prayer. Keep reading. Go on, turn the page and Shine!!!

December 4th

Do you have a "to do" list and a "not want to do" list? Today I'm on the "not wanting to do" list. My bathroom needs cleaning, and my laundry needs washing. To be frank, I don't feel like doing it! In our house, we've been watching THE CROWN on TV. Yes, that crowd carries a ton of responsibility. But can you imagine walking away from your bed and someone will make it? Or walking away from dirty dishes and 'wallah' someone picks them up? When GOD handed out positions on that train, perhaps I was in the caboose. Kids, it's one of those days. Geronimo, here I go. Hey, I don't have to beat the clothes on a rock. Also, the outhouse is in the house. I know, Steve, quit your whining and get with it. The sooner you do it, the sooner you will Shine!!!

Footnote: What makes a person's life successful? I think neither wealth, power nor fame. Discovering the purpose God created us for is sometimes a mystery. Perhaps it is right in front of our noses. It is important to SHINE in the light of our glorious creator. Why? Because God made us to know Him, love Him and serve Him. Now I cannot tell you what your purpose is. YOU must search for your answer. And when you find it, you will SHINE!!!

December 6th a.m.

Some look upon GOD as this awesome (which He is) supreme being. But for me, He's my very best friend. Now I do not pray in elaborate mystical ways. Rather, it's a daily, sometimes minute-to-minute dialog. I take Him with me most everywhere, and I'm ever so honest. Why not? He knows everything about me. Why waste time being a pretender? (LIKE MOST OF US DO WHEN PRESENTING OURSELVES TO OTHERS.) Save your breath. GOD hears, sees, and knows everything. And He is available to everyone - even the worst of the worst. There is a slang saying, "Don't get your panties in a wad." I will say that about this time. God has got it covered, kids. Yes, be on guard, but don't lose your integrity. HE has our backs. Give Him thanks every day and try to do your best, just like I am doing here. No great sermon; it's my style. Me being me, feeling awesome when I SHINE!!!

December 6th p.m.

Oh yes, here I go again. Someone was giving out bona fide facts. Another person told me to listen to this well-educated person. They know a lot about the subject. No argument with that; education is the first step to gain knowledge and critical thinking. But don't you think there is also immense value to simple common sense? I'm not always impressed by this degree or that degree. A diploma may have put them in the driver's seat. Never mistake the person in the backseat! They see things from the roadside the driver never catches sight of. Albert Einstein said, "Education is what remains after one has forgotten what one has learned in school." E=MC2; his brilliance SHINES on!!!

December 7th a.m.

Still dark outside here in paradise. A light rain has been falling for hours. I've already worked out at the gym. When I got home, I sat in my truck for a few minutes, listening to the raindrops on the roof - a sound I love, but love even better in my nice warm house! Today's weather report: cold front on the way. I can hear people complaining already, telling me, "This is not what I came to Florida for." I'd like to say, "Didn't you come here to experience everything: sunny, cloudy, rainy and - perhaps for a short period - cold days? No use complaining over something we have no control over. Learn to adapt." Many years ago, I lived farther north, and for a year I experienced a colder climate. The worst of it was dressing up in winter attire. I don't care for layers of this and that. Here, most of the year, I wear shorts and tee shirts. I kept my old postal sweater, and it does the trick when it's cold in the Sunshine State. Not what you might call fashionable, and something tells me I'll never be on the best dressed list. Wherever you live, try to find something special about your day. Rain or SHINE!!!

December 7th p.m.

There is nothing compared to the healing power of a simple touch. Now that I'm retired (5 years), I'm working a simple job requiring simple touches. Many people have touched my heart, even though I had never met most of them before. It's amazing how in just a few minutes, with words and sight, our lives touch each other's soul. I am surprised by what I've learned about people in these brief series of special moments. Sometimes we share private thoughts - and, I might add, kept guarded - such an unexpected gift that I never imagined would become part of my life. This past year has put a strain on my experiences. Masks block the interactions to a great extent. They create a 'wall', and it makes it hard to hear. Masks hide facial expressions like smiles and frowns. Looks speak volumes without words. Most dislike the masks. And touching has become a no-no! I understand. Masks are creating shadow people. A veil covers what we once saw. Sadness has cloaked planet Earth. It's difficult to live; it's difficult to breathe. I miss the hugs, the personal touch from one soul to the other. Like the lyrics in the 1972 ABBA song, "People need hope, people need loving." We must find a way within our masked lives to say, "I wish you love, hope and happiness." Reach out and touch someone's life by showing you care. Be courteous. Don't get impatient in the parking lot. Stop for people in the cross walks. SHINE in any way you can, and it will help banish the black clouds!!!

December 8th

I used to think 65 was so ancient. Now my ship is heading towards that port. Heck, I am only in second gear! And what a wonderful time, too. I've learned so much and value all the things life has taught me. It's funny, my boys consider me an antique, but heck, I'm at the gym four days a week and still working part- time. Yes, the cover of my book may look a bit weathered, but new exciting chapters are ahead on the horizon. I plan to SHINE all the way to the harbor!!!

Footnote: Momentous news today! In the UK, a 90-year-old woman received the first dose of the coronavirus vaccine. "Go for it," she said, encouraging others to get the vaccine. The U.S. hopes to get the vaccine approved very soon!!!

December 9th

Remember, no man is a failure who has friends! This message came from a classic movie, "It's a Wonderful Life." And true to my heart, I often write about being thankful. So much of that comes with being blessed to surround myself with genuine friends. Anyone can be an acquaintance, but it takes a special person to become a friend. One of our greatest gifts is having a good, loyal friend, a person who sees everything about you - close up - and still has your back. When you have a TRUE friend, BINGO - YOU WON THE LOTTERY! Make this a spectacular day, MY FRIENDS. NOW get out there and SHINE!!

December 10th

The Woman Behind The Green Door. My first piece of real estate was a simple two- bedroom duplex. I sold my beloved car to put the down payment on it. In this development there were two exterior colors, and the doors were chocolate brown. Well not ALL the doors. A kind, older woman loved the color green; not just any green, but olive green. Her car and her carpets were olive green, and rumors circulated that her cat was dyed olive green. Well, all hell broke out, and the board called a meeting to order when she painted her door her favorite color. The hammer came down; paint brushes came out. Like a famous lady who once screamed, "NO WIRE HANGERS," the governing board shrieked, "No olive-green doors!" Of course, the association had the paperwork to prove it. You know me: I said, "Oh, let her have her door." They deemed me "out of order!" Anyway, it was at that moment I realized I couldn't hack this garb. I wanted to live in a place free of rules and regulations. Yes, friends, we live in a world of rules and regulations. I think many rules are necessary. Can't say I always like them. Yesterday there was a discussion about whether wearing a mask helps to thwart the virus. Some people believe that masks do not protect you from the virus; it's a plot. Do I enjoy wearing a mask? No. But it's necessary out of respect for our fellow man. Today, the woman behind the green door popped into my mind. If she is still around, I can bet you know what color her mask is! But did you know that olive green represents the traditional color of peace? Shine on in olive green, friends!!!

Footnote: Last night we received breaking news on the TV! The FDA has authorized emergency use of one of the coronavirus vaccines in the U.S. Fed Ex and UPS trucks should be rolling out soon.

December 12th a.m.

There is a rather witty, famous, talented woman who once said, "I've been poor, and I've been rich; rich is better." I love this true rubber-meets-the-road statement. Being poor sucks; I understand that gig. 2020 has been a troublesome time for those trying to make ends meet. It's heartbreaking. So rather than deciding who to blame, turn your hearts to giving. There are philanthropic organizations such as children's hospitals, veterans' organizations, animal charities and local soup kitchens/food banks. Even small donations add up! Don't have money to spare? Find other ways to "pay it forward" with good deeds. Help a friend in need or write a thank you note to someone you appreciate. SHINE (from the bottom of your heart) and make the world a better place!!!

December 12th p.m.

In my neighborhood, more and more younger families are moving in. I am ever so happy that many homes are decorated with beautiful lights. People drive by to look at them. The spirit of Christmas is alive and well in this most wonderful time of the year! Cherish every moment. Take it slow and easy if you can. There are so many distractions out there. Put them on hold and let your spirit's soar. Adopt a joyful attitude. "Come, they told me, pa-rum-pum-pum-pum. A newborn King to see..." Shine on, little drummer boy!!!

December 13th

"Change the World" … A favorite song by a popular recording artist sums up my thoughts. What a fractured world we live in. 2020 rolled in like a steamroller and then turned upside down. On top of everything, in the political world, bitter fighting continues. Enough is enough! We need to be on our best behavior. So how do we change the world? In my small part of this world, I plan to practice random acts of kindness. So MAKE a pledge. Open the doors to your heart and close your mouth to hurtful words. "If I could reach the stars, I'd pull one down for you. SHINE it on my heart. So you could see the truth…"

Footnote: "Change the World" is a song written by Tommy Sims, Gordon Kennedy, and Wayne Kirkpatrick, and recorded by Eric Clapton for the soundtrack of the 1996 film, "Phenomenon."

December 14th

We can gain strength from recognizing our weaknesses. Pride is the ultimate destroyer. It blinds us from acknowledging our flaws and stunts our growth. Everyone has shortcomings. Perhaps one of our purposes on earth is to grow by overcoming obstacles. My prayer is... Dear GOD, help us snuff out pride, humble ourselves and SHINE in your glory!!!

Footnote: Some are calling it "D-Day" or "V- Day." Historical, yes, as the U.S. rolls out the long-awaited vaccinations. Healthcare workers will be among the first to be vaccinated.

December 16th

One special thing I enjoy doing is working with the public. I love people. I've been working jobs that involve customer service most of my life, but it's not always roses and daffodils. When I worked for the postal service, there were tough days. The public has no idea how demanding it can be for a mail carrier. Often, we had to split a route. It involved doing our own route and also covering another person's route. This story is a beaut! Remember, the clock ticks fast when you have bundles of mail to deliver. My motto: Move it, move it, move it! On my route, the road was long. In the distance, I saw a little man waving his arms. The closer I came, the louder he screamed. He looked like a carbon copy of Louie from the television series "Taxi" - small, rotund, wild hair, and wilder mouth. He was calling me every name in the book. Most of them had the 'F' bomb attached. He announced I was "the worst mailman he'd ever met." Then a voice in my head said, "Keep your cool, Warren. You can't make everyone happy." I think young people should spend a year working with the public. It could be an invaluable experience with human nature. I've met so many wonderful people along the way. And then along came Louie. Well, you can't win them all. So try to Shine whatever the day brings!!!

December 17th

One thing special about Christmas is the lights. There is something magical about seeing them illuminate the darkness. And even more important, the light that comes from within when we show our true colors. Once, I had a scrooge-like neighbor. At Christmas time, he would decorate his house with lights, and holiday paraphernalia would garnish his lawn. I know we cannot - nor should we - judge anyone, but don't walk on his lawn or you'll regret it! Strictly for show. To me, it's a no-go. Your light and your love should come out every day of the year. Do you know a lighthouse has a powerful bright light on the top called a beacon? It helps sailors guide their ships at night. Just like the star on the top of a Christmas tree, it represents HOPE. SHINE on, weary travelers; there is light at the end of the tunnel!!!

December 18th

There was a report in the news this morning about someone placing a gold coin worth thousands of dollars in the Salvation Army bucket. Not surprising to me because I believe in the Christmas Spirit. Perhaps in our fallen nature, the delusion whispers…This journey is all about you. Nope, not even close. Humanity failed that lesson from day two. God created us to interact with our brothers and our sisters - all colors, shapes and beliefs - and to experience life with appreciation as we share the gifts God gave us. Do you feel something special when you help someone? Joy emanating within your heart? I do, and it's not a fluke either. It exists some place inside of us. Life can place layer upon layer of burdens on our hearts, and sometimes we become lost. I recall a news story about an abandoned baby someone left at a shelter. Many people reached out and sent donations to help the child. In God's book, GOOD people outnumber the bad. Shed the layers of overloads in your heart so your LOVE can SHINE through!!!

Footnote: Keep love in your heart. A life without it is like a sunless garden when the flowers are dead. The consciousness of loving and being loved brings warmth and a richness to life that nothing else can bring. - Oscar Wilde

December 19th

Another beautiful day; another beautiful night. Maybe it's the pandemic, but I have a rage to live. Trying to get 'everything in.' Don't want to miss a moment. Friends, don't take a second for granted. Life is like riding a fast- moving train. Me, I'm at the window trying to take in all the scenery. Zip, zip, zip, so goes our time on earth. Find beauty in the day; nightfall comes in a blink of an eye. Silent night, holy night. SHINE on as we proclaim the Savior's birth!!!

December 21st

This is the season for WISHING! So what are you hoping for? In the past, I have longed for certain things to happen, and also wished that certain things had never happened. Friends, the best thing about a new day is it's a clean slate, without limitations to wish for whatever you want. As I began growing older, my wish list changed. Oh yes, from material items to spiritual things that live in the heart. I sometimes struggle with the 'what has happened list,' between my downfalls, poor decisions and/or what fate laid on my table. We have no power over the past, so step forward and re-write what you can do about the present. In quiet moments, I put things in my prayer list to God, and I want to add you, the reader, to my list. I hope that you find character values in each day. Our psyches gravitate toward the things we place importance on. Wishes in our hearts are ever so important. Keep them going; own them, visualize them. You are only a wish away from reality if you believe. My prayers go out to each of you as we SHINE through the holiday season!!!

Footnote: It's the first day of winter and a second drug company's vaccine is ready for distribution. Coronavirus cases continue to spike in the U.S. and around the world. A mutated strain of the virus hit the UK and is spreading rapidly. Buckle your seat belts, friends; we are still in for a heck of a ride as the new year approaches. Remember keep the faith; hope can and will outshine any darkness!

December 23rd

Are you grateful for the people GOD has sent into your life?

Often, individuals come into our lives for reasons and sometimes just for a season. Get out your magic mirror and you will see a 'pattern' of reasons. No, not everyone you meet will be that admirable person, but there is a divine reason. Friends, I've failed this 'master class' many times. I've had to re-take the course many times, too. I smile, thinking about the friends in my life. I have a practical friend who can be honest with me. Another positive friend who encourages me. And there are many who have to reel in my 'wild' thoughts. Yes, the wheels on my brain turn round and round. I love all my friends. They are 'presents' under my tree of life. Appreciate your friends and you will SHINE!!!

Footnote: Romper Room was a children's television show. It aired 1953 through 1994. The hostess of the show would look through a 'magic mirror' and recite the rhyme: "Romper, bomper, stomper boo. Tell me, tell me, tell me do." So tell me, are you SHINING today?

December 24th

Dear friends, we live in an age where our government has many programs to help this group or aid that group. Some are fantastic, some are not. Most problems come from the human heart. Greed and power lay inside many hearts today. It is part of the 'ME' generation. Success dictates our status, the homes we live in and the cars we drive. I'll agree if you work hard, you deserve these things. But they are things. I am reaching the age where I find my toy box is full of trinkets and rewards. Or so I thought. One day, God will call my name. My 'stuff' might appear in a thrift store, or on the curb waiting for the garbage man. Precious things in the heart become more and more important. Treat those in your path with kindness, offer moments of encouragement for the downtrodden, and show empathy to a stranger. These are my plans of action. Allow them to become yours. I am working at the simplest job in my lifetime. I serve the public and have never felt such meaning and responsibility. How I treat a stranger may be part of God's eternal purpose. Even one kind act can change a heart and give hope in a darkened world. Life is moving fast into eternity for a lot of us. This moment will never occur again. Open your hearts; do good to others. And keep an open mind. You never know how important you are. A light appears when you SHINE, allowing you to view the path ahead.

December 26th

Christmas day has come and gone along with the preparations, anxiety, & fanfare. But it is not all about Christmas decorations and celebrations. No, not at all. It's about the precious gift God gives… the gift of a child. I thought I knew everything about raising a child when my first son arrived. In reality, I did not. I discovered it is a learn-as-you-go experience. If I could do it over, would I change anything? Yes. Some things that I deemed important were not. My children are my special blessings, but the most remarkable gift GOD has ever given anyone is His only begotten Son, Jesus, born in a lowly manger, raised by a young humble mother and kind earthly foster father. Jesus was only 33 when He died on the cross for our sins. Now God's Son is the King of the Universe and our stellar light in the darkness! Let His light SHINE in your hearts!!!

December 28th a.m.

A picture of my great grandfather sits on my bedroom dresser. I bear an uncanny resemblance to him and his eyes look right at me. Perhaps a little spooky? But I value the memorabilia of my ancestor. One hears people say they can't wait to ring in a new year. Out with the old, in with the new. And it is not surprising that this year it has become a mantra. Yes, a year like no other! But I recall a story my father told me when he was a young man and his family moved to Florida. His older brother, William, ran ahead of their truck with a lantern to light the way on the road at night. Yup, they lived in primitive standards. I'm talking about out-houses, kerosene lanterns, washing clothes by hand and hanging them out to dry, and – gulp - no air conditioning. And living through WWII must have been daunting: the economy was tough, supplies were scarce. Americans made sacrifices. Many soldiers lost their lives. Then a couple decades later, the Vietnam war staked its claim on soldiers' lives. Quite a few veterans came home with disabilities and PTSD. Now some people are unhappy about having to wear a mask while shopping! And then they return to their homes equipped with all the modern conveniences. Friends, we have experienced some dire straits in 2020. But despite it all, we are a blessed people! Who knows when we can stop using masks? Will life return to what we deemed normal? Now is an awesome place to be. Today I'm here; I walk, talk, see and enjoy the moment. It's not the mask, but what's underneath it that counts! Perhaps someday my picture (though faded) might be on a next generation family member's dresser. Will they wonder what my lifetime was like? Maybe they will read my book and get a glimpse of what my life was like during the pandemic? I hope they will SHINE no matter what life brings their way!!!

December 28th

Hope flourishes with a vengeance as workers on the front lines are being given the vaccine. I don't understand, but I sense little positivity out in the public domain. More distressing is when some one's psychological outlook causes them to distance themselves from others. We are tittering in the crossroads, treading water in a pool, not quite ready to swim to the steps yet. I can say this: staying home within our walls is no way to live. It's like receiving a present and keeping it in the box. God created us to enjoy each other's company. For now, I remain behind a mask. Can't say that I buy into the conspiracy theory, but I don't like the 'government always knows best' group either. This weekend I took my family to visit a blast from the past: a famous street lined with stores where the upper crust shop. The crowds appeared like an abstract painting, passing each other on the street with masks on. It was if it was an episode from "The Twilight Zone." Still, the sounds and sights of the holiday decorations lifted my spirits, and I felt a deep sense of relief. Although it was a cool day, the sun was in mid-sky, spreading its warmth. Later the moon rose, casting its light in the black sky. Count-down week for the ball to drop in Times Square. Ready to "look over the fence?" Hope there aren't vicious dogs hanging out on the other side! SHINING with eyes open, ears listening, and a grateful heart!!!

December 30th

Driving home from the gym, an old tune blasted on the radio. I was on the edge of seventeen when I first heard this song. Youth was exhilarating as I headed to work in my first car. Anyone remember the saying, "If I could go back knowing what I know now, but chances are I wouldn't be the person I am today?" I'm supposed to be where I am now. Life experiences made me who I am. As I parked my truck, I smiled, then I toasted the young man I once was. Here's looking at you, kid! And to the older gentleman I've become? Don't forget to SHINE Warren; you're on overtime!!!

December 31st

Today is the last day of 2020. The calendar tells us this ending will become a new beginning. Friends, I cannot count how many times I've experienced endings and beginnings. Life in a nutshell: The sun comes up; the moon replaces it. We lose a small part of us and gain another. Often, I've felt like I have re-invented myself a few times. Inside, my heart longs for so many things to happen. Life keeps us going. Resolutions will help you map the course. I make them every day to keep on track. Humans are subject to flaws. Some we can fix; others are a work in progress. Has this year been the worst ever? Not for me. I've been through terrible times and survived by the skin of my teeth. We're still here, doing what we need to do, wishing for a better year. Just another day on the calendar. When the sun comes up, we'll get another 'crack' at it. I am ever so positive. Happy New Year! SHINE ON with the resilience you showed in 2020!!!

Epilogue

The coronavirus first emerged in Wuhan, China late in 2019. In January 2020, the United States reported the onset of a few cases. Months went by and heart-rending news circulated in the media. Colored graphs pointed out the rising numbers of the virus in the states. Photos of hospital staff suited up, and patients on ventilators in the ICU emerged to depict the seriousness of the situation. At the end of the year, there were (approximately) 83 million cases: 47 million people recovered, and 1.8 million people died around the world. Life appeared to exist in a bubble. People had to wear masks, cities canceled public events, shutdowns occurred, and depletion of supplies fueled the fire! But HOPE survived despite everything! Recently, the vaccine became available for front-line employees in the U.S. Now it's becoming available for people over 65. Yes, the light at the end of the tunnel is much brighter!!!

Hello 2021

I treasure today more than I ever have. If I'm going on a picnic and it rains…I'll eat in the car and try to enjoy a delightful conversation. Living with what comes. Life brings laughter, tears, celebrations and yes, times when we grieve. Friends, wouldn't it be great if we could 'design' all of our days? Silk and satin, but without thorns along the way. I can remember as a child thinking what the year 2000 would   be like. A cartoon show called 'The Jetsons" made me wonder if we'd have flying cars and live on other planets. Younger people might laugh but my grandparents never imagined microwaves, flat-screen TV's and iPhones. Offer me a crystal ball to see what this year will bring, and I wouldn't want to look. How can I enjoy today if I'm busy glimpsing into tomorrow? No predictions or forecasts in my mind. One day at a time. We've become fast- forward people, wishing and planning for the future but forgetting the simple value of a day. My heart is thankful to be here in 2021. Like a newborn baby, my slate is clean. Reflect on a verse from Isaiah 40:31: "But those who hope in the LORD will renew their strength. They will soar on wings like eagles; they will run and not grow weary; they will walk and not be faint."

Yes, friends, 2020 was a strange, difficult, stressful year, jam-packed with anxiety and fear. But within the layers of my heart, a tiny light of serenity exists. I pray and believe that   it will grow stronger. I know God loves us and will not leave us without HOPE! Anchor your faith in the arms of our loving Father who is the Great I Am! Walk with courage and determination into the new year believing there will be ample opportunities to SHINE!!!

Also by Steve Warren:

Conversations From The Porch

Conversations From the Porch is an inspirational book compromised of Steve's thoughts. He shares the ups and downs of everyday life, while encouraging his readers to SHINE, even on rainy days.